a storehouse of tales

CONTEMPORARY INDIAN WOMEN WRITERS

a storehouse of tales

CONTEMPORARY INDIAN WOMEN WRITERS

Edited by

Jehanara Wasi

Introduction by

Malashri Lal

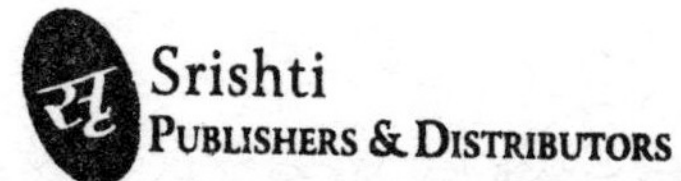
Srishti
Publishers & Distributors

SRISHTI PUBLISHERS & DISTRIBUTORS
64-A, Adhchini
Sri Aurobindo Marg
New Delhi 110017
First published by SRISHTI PUBLISHERS & DISTRIBUTORS in 2001

Rs.195.00
ISBN 81-87075-35-X

Cover Design by Arrt Creations
45 Nehru Apartment, Kalkaji, New Delhi 110 019
e-mail: arrt@vsnl.com

Printed and bound in India by
Saurabh Print-O-Pack
A-16, Sector IV, Noida

Contents

Introduction

Malashri Lal

Once upon a time there was a grandmother, spartan and thin, a bundle of energy in the kitchen, a storm of words in the zenana, a storehouse of tales in the bedroom. As dusk gathered its golden strands and passed into amorphous darkness, this grandmother discovered her power in language in the stories she told – innumerable, undocumented, intuitive creations – her rich quilt of memory and social comment.

Despite cable TV, Dolby sound systems, computer graphics and other wonders of cyberspace, the grandmother as storyteller survives as a trope of Indian culture even if she is often physically transformed or even absent. For women in India are born to storytelling. Even as they imbibe, absorb, the circumstances of their mundane, everyday lives, they create alternate and frequently, better worlds in their fecund imagination. Like Emily Dickinson, they might "tell all the truth but tell it slant" or like Mahasweta Devi make it a mission to document "history in the making." One way or another, the woman storyteller has offered a different dimension to civil society than men have.

At one time this contrast would have marked a difference in subject matter that women write of interior and domestic spaces and men write about the public domain. While there was considerable truth about this perceived division of literary subjects even upto the 1980s in Indian English writing, such distribution is no longer visible, nor is it at all desirable. Remembering the contexts of history and society operative for Toru Dutt and Sarojini Naidu in colonial times, one can understand their acceptance of the limits placed upon their literary expression. That women writers in post colonial times, including the famous trio, Kamala Markandaya, Anita Desai and Nayantara Sahgal, tended to tread softly on radical grounds is a fact widely acknowledged. Yet, their novels and stories were not endorsing tradition. If one read carefully, the womanist strategy of a masked protest, a thoughtful, sometimes anguished questioning of patriarchal conditions came to the fore. There was, however, a compromise, a timidity which prevented most of the earlier writers from declaring a feminist position even if critics pointed clearly to the texts which were challenging social constructions inimical to women.

Perhaps the problem lay with the term "feminist" or even the African-American modification, "womanist." In the debates in India during the 1970s and 1980s it was repeatedly asserted that the terms and their reference were "western" and therefore unusable outside their originary context. Local, cultural vocabulary such as "nariwad" or "narithwa" were suggested from Hindi but somehow, did not gain currency. Yet *Manushi* flourished as a forum for Indian women, and India's first feminist press, Kali for Women, gained prominence. Meanwhile theoretical formulations on feminism, especially from the USA and France, began to show an influential presence in Indian academia although there was a growing resistance to using western frameworks to "fit" around Indian texts. Within these volatile discussions, worldwide, about "What is Feminism?," another fissure opened up, unexpectedly, between writers and critics. Highly reputed women novelists from several countries disclaimed any allegiance to the underscored category of "women writers" emphasizing that the creative imagination could not be split by gender. Margaret Atwood in Canada, Doris Lessing in Britain, Nadine Gordimer in South Africa and Anita Desai and Shashi Deshpande in India may be counted among them.

Some aspects of these vital debates have subsided, while others persist. The present collection of stories would be enriched if contextualised within a discussion about literary issues today. In an obvious declaration of separateness, the anthology foregrounds women writers, to which there is the subtext that women have a gendered voice. Manju Kapur's *Chocolate* is a fine example of revenge and reversal uniquely using tools available to women in adverse circumstances. This story along with a few others (*Cry, My Beloved Child, Bhadoo*) locates the site of discourse on the woman's body, the only space she can hope to claim as her own.

Understanding the intricate functions and emotions of this femaleness, the writers speak of its moods, its desires, its protests and submissions.

The woman as writer, as creatrix, is another subject this collection addresses, which again challenges an old idea that men are creative, women are procreative; or in book-market words, "Men are from Mars and Women are from Venus." Well, are they? At least two stories here (*A Toast to Herself* and *Simone de Beauvoir and the Manes*) argue for the honour of the woman writer's profession and refuse to see it, as Indian society often does, as an unfortunate phase of dabbling with words, an excess of fancy to be cured by a "suitable" marriage. Since I spoke earlier about Indian feminism's link with ideological developments worldwide, it is worth noting that on the aspects of the body and the role of the writer, the premises of argument bear similarity with statements made elsewhere. Susan Gubar and Sandra Gilbert showed how the woman writer inscribes her own "madness" into her imaginative fiction, Margaret Atwood thought up the image of the "edible woman" devoured by an unthinking male companion, the French feminists focussed on *ecriture feminine* based on the structure of the female body.

Along with such common ground co-exists a great deal of literary material that is specific to India. Susie Tharu and K. Lalita in the two volumes *Women Writing in India: 600 B.C. to the Present* set out to map "the practices of the self or agency and of narrative that emerge at the contested margins of patriarchy, empire, and nation." Contemporary writers, featured in the present collection, show a sensitivity to the transitions that are changing the face of the post-independence nation in terms of class and caste. Bulbul Sharma's *Anadi's Journey*, Madhu Kishwar's *Twenty or Twenty-Five*? and Shama Futehally's *Jani's Morning* take us into the interiors of a cityscape or the corners of a rural hamlet to pause at the doorstep of new vistas and new values to interrogate the nature of the change from tradition to modernity. And it is not a clear trajectory they notice.

There is humour too for the woman writer is not necessarily an enumerator of miseries. Namita Gokhale's story is about the romps of a female yuppie in Rishikesh; Anuradha Marwah Roy smiles at the self-indulgent complacency of the bored housewife.

What happened to the old pictics about "motherhood" and "son preference" that featured so prominently in earlier discourses on cultural leanings in India? Mrinal Pande's thoughtful, compassionate voice reflects upon the idea of the maternal with the critical shifts in youthful thinking today.

India, that playful land of contradictions, is well expressed by the contrast in the tales told by the "beloved witch," Ipsita Roy Chakraverti, and the social activist Manju Kak. The magic of Wicca peers past the glorious edifices of Lutyens' Delhi to reveal essences of evil sunk deep into the foundations of the city's wealth and power. Kak takes us to another India of hill folks, superstitions, a new found nationalism heady with brute strength. Madhu Tandan adds that touch of the inexplicable to the common routine.

India, celebrating fifty years of independence, offered to the audience a haunting remake of "Vande Mataram." India entered the new millennium singing paeans to information technology. India's writers, from Rushdie to Roy, spanned the diversity of a nation which refuses to be defined by any consistent image. A taste of this diversity is contained in this anthology of short stories. As changeable as the monsoon sky, as exhilarating as a ride on a village swing, as taut as the kite strings at Makar Sankranti, as demanding of attention as the Ring Road traffic, these stories capture today's assertions – and yesterday's nostalgia.

Delhi: City of the Dead

Ipsita Roy Chakraverti

People often ask me what evil is. They feel I should know. Maybe they're right. I've seen the workings of strange and hostile forces wreaking their will on living beings and I have wondered if that is evil. I've witnessed people confounded by that which they cannot put a name to – and I have asked myself if this is the other face of good. Where does one end and the other begin? Good and Evil – a being with two faces – strangely enough, looking in the same direction. Like an oriental deity, possessed of many arms but one soul. And from that soul, like molten lava, streams forth the power which takes a path, a way, through darkness or light. We are taught that we should walk the lighted way – but oh, the beauty of darkness, when all the senses come alive.

In the course of my work with Wicca and the working of men's minds I have come across complex puzzles and mazes when trying to decipher what men call good and what they label evil. "Evil" is what they do not understand, that which seduces them and taunts them and lurks in the mist of their minds. "Good" is what they have found in well thumbed scripture books and is well scrubbed and intolerably antiseptic and it does not cause discomfort to their conditioned convictions.

But whether they will or not – evil lives on. Where? Amongst many other places, it lives where men have once trod. It persists in places where he has loved and lusted and killed others and himself. Insidiously, silently, it creeps into the present from a not so forgotten past and makes its presence felt. Such is its nature and such is its power.

I once delved into the secrets of places which people call evil and haunted and I stumbled upon truths which amazed. I discovered that often the darkest forces can lurk beneath the greenest grass. A freshly painted wicket fence may conceal the macabre. I wished to probe the haunted sites and houses of this fair capital of India – Delhi. For I had been led to believe that Delhi is home to some of the most sinister plots that I would ever come across in a career devoted to the supernatural and the unexplained. This is of course, a deliberate play on words, for I do not refer to the conspiracies and assassinations and bloodbaths that have led to the seats of power in Delhi. Generations of invaders have stormed this place and intrigued and killed and ruled and have been slain. Blood has seeped into this land and the spreading, old trees here have tasted of it. The grandest fort here, is made of red stone. Is it to celebrate the blood which has been shed for power? This hungry land, soaked with yearning and lust does not sleep – and it is a land, ready to devour and strike, if disturbed. But, in the course of time, men forget and do turn the old soil to make way for the new And that is when the restless dead arise…and walk again on this paradise on earth.

There are many fair properties which consist of Lutyens' Delhi. The government's bungalows for its very important persons, and the verdant colonies with flats for its bureaucrats. There they nestle, surrounded by high walls and lush lawns. There, every night, sleep the country's rulers and policy-makers – in the arms of those who have not really departed.

How many know that many of the city's present official residences stand where erstwhile residents had lain down – albeit unwillingly – in the hope of final peace? In making way for the new, graveyards or kabaristans have been disturbed. And such disturbances release hostile and darkened waves from the earth, which rise with the heat and dust of Delhi's gruelling summers and the cold mists of winter, seeking to vent their anger on the living.

A former Solicitor-General of India, a man of learning and worldly wisdom and with little time for whims or flights of fancy had a strange experience to relate. During his sojourn at number 8 Krishna Menon Marg, some years back, he would often be awakened during the early hours of the morning, by an undefinable chill and a feeling that there was someone else in the bedroom apart from his sleeping wife and himself. It was eerie. It was 4 a.m. one morning in October, when he suddenly woke up. It was almost as if somebody shook him awake. The room was in semi-darkness and a strange mist was gathering at the foot of his bed. Then he could gradually see the face and figure of an old, bearded man, in white robes, who stood and observed him with glazed eyes, for what seemed to Mr. G., a very long while. Then the apparition turned and crossed the room silently, towards the window. Mr. G's wife slept on. He did not mention the incident to her. A few nights later, however it was she who shook him awake and cried out that she had had a strange dream. She talked of having seen a man in a white robe. An old Muslim holy man, she said. Mr. G. saw this entity a few more times before political changes took place and he felt it expedient to move.

Who is this disturbed entity at number 8 Krishna Menon Marg? Can anyone ever be truly happy or content there? I went to investigate the place once, just before Mr. G. left. Perhaps he was happy enough while he was there, but the point is that circumstances did not allow him to enjoy his position or the house for very long. When I last saw him in that house, he was sitting, a bit forlornly in his study, overseeing the packing of heavy legal books into cartons. A wispy shape overlooked the details.

There is a bungalow on Motilal Nehru Marg, whose entrance is placed at an odd 30 degrees to the main road. It is number 3 and the bungalow needed a facelift when I last saw it. However the member of parliament and his wife who occupy it, have made it comfortable within. Still, whenever I have been there, I have felt eerie eyes watching and waiting – for something to happen. Each gust of wind sets up a weird rustle in the old trees outside. I feel that in spite of its smiling green gardens, the earth forces there are sinister. Strangely enough, sooner or later they seem to affect the hearts and fortunes of the man of the house. Former Congress heavyweight Arun Nehru, lived there at one time. He suffered a massive heart attack. His fortunes declined. Former Congress Union Minister, Jaffer Sharief lived there too. His heart problems came later, but he could not escape the curse. Strange rumours abounded while he lived there. Some said he kept camels on the grounds, which he had served up on the dining table when the fancy struck him. The house started getting a bizarre reputation. People said it brought no good to its occupants. And strangely enough the present resident, even though he divides his time between there and his own flat on Aurangzeb Road, has been suffering from cardiac problems. His career has seen frustrations. He was an ambitious man.

I personally experienced and witnessed the strange goings on at Block E, Sector 13 of Ramakrishna Puram. I moved into a lovely, sunny, ground floor flat in the summer of 1993. It seemed spacious, welcoming and smelled of fresh paint. There were two verandahs on either side. One overlooked the kitchen garden, where winter saw a profusion of tomatoes, carrots and cabbages. The other verandah, was enclosed by ornamental wrought iron grills and a door which led onto a huge lawn which remained green even at the height of a Delhi summer. There were a few flowering trees in white and yellow and I planted a gardenia bush which bloomed almost immediately. All seemed well. The first week was busy but uneventful. But from the second week onwards, there was no denying it.

I would frequently hear loud thumps outside as a heavy weight or a body falling on hard ground. Practically every morning, between 4.30 a.m. and 5 a.m. there would be scraping sounds of furniture being dragged across the room, emanating from the floor above. This would continue even when the flat above fell vacant. Tentative taps on closet doors was a common feature. Once or twice, at dusk, I caught glimpses of a woman shrouded in grey, near a bougainvillaea bush. At such times, my dog would start to bark uncontrollably – even though investigations outside revealed nothing amiss.

Then something happened to further rouse my suspicions about the block. An officer and his wife had moved into a flat on the sixth floor. Within a month, they were out of there in a panic. Not much was divulged but rumours went that the lady, normally a very practical and cheerful wife, was unable to tolerate the inexplicable gloom and sense of impending doom in that flat. Some said she started to have morbid hallucinations. Anyhow, without stopping to find out what was causing those chilling disturbances the couple fled from there and chose to put up with the relative discomfort of a transit flat. The irony lies in the fact that evil generally shows a charming face – maybe to entice and beguile. And Block E of R.K. Puram is certainly charming. A quiet, tree lined road leads upto it. In summer it drips with golden laburnum and in autumn with some sweet smelling blossoms I could never put a name to. Drive down there on an evening, when you have nothing else to do.

I did ask some old residents about the background of that site or that building. An elderly maid who worked for me said that many people there kept hearing sounds in the evening. Then in hushed tones she reported that about five years ago, a woman who worked for a family on the sixth floor had fallen to her death.

'How?' I asked. 'Was it an accident?'

'No, many people said it wasn't,' she answered grimly. 'But who's to know what goes on behind doors?' She left it at that but added, maybe as an afterthought, 'The land here has a curse. These curses never die. They make people do bad things. Who's to say whose fault it really all is?' Very profound, I thought.

Was it the same curse that dogged the house across the way from Block E? A certain Union Minister, an erstwhile ruler from a princely state, chose to build a marble mansion for his daughters in that very area. It was a strange, huge house with very few windows. A journalist once commented that it looked like a mausoleum. However it was nobody's business what a house chose to look like. But it was true that the house seemed to take a long while to complete. The minister soon started ruling. He retired from public life. His daughters moved into the gift from their father. Soon before I moved away from R.K. Puram I heard of a dreadful tragedy in that very house. One of the sons-in-law, started suffering from depression there. He ended it by shooting himself.

There are other places in Delhi, haunted and sinister. Houses built near mazaars or burial places. Come to think of it, Delhi's like one huge graveyard, where the living and the dead sit side by side and dine and wonder at how dreams and desires never really die. The lust for gold and power still stalks the land and turns to exhilarating evil. And of course, evil never rests.

In Kaka Nagar stands a guest house which faces a mazaar. There is another old tomb across the road from it. Old survey maps say that at one time long ago, kabaristans extended from Sujan Singh Park right upto Purana Qila. But to return to the guest house, there are no ghosts here that I have seen or heard. But those who have sojourned within its rooms, complain of peculiar shifts in personality. Meaning that the worst and the weakest in them, inexplicably comes to the fore. 'Thoughts which I would never entertain at other times, or at all, seemed to overtake me there,' said somebody who did not wish to be named.

I spent a few nights within its walls. I wished to experience its ambience. It was some time in early April and the garden in front, was wilting but still pleasing to the eye, with late blooming petunias and marigold. I occupied a suite on the ground floor. It was well appointed and furnished with the usual comforts—but a trifle chilly. I don't think it was my imagination, but I definitely felt swirls of cold air there, in different areas at different times. The nights were restful till about 3 a.m., when something would disturb and prompt one to get up and go into the small living area. There, the air would be heavy with something, I can only label as sadness. I would sit down with deliberate detachment and with the air of an observer. I was aware of the unfriendly, resentful currents criss-crossing the room. One night, from the bedroom, I heard the sound of voices raised in argument coming from the adjoining room. Of course there was nobody there. The only sign of alien presences was in the shape of a broken glass which lay on the floor. I do not know who could have knocked it down. It seemed to have been smashed against the door. I also marked the fact that the staff were not too keen to stay late. This I at first put down to the common laziness of those who serve, but then I noticed that at other times they were relatively hardworking and attentive. However, as evening approached they were eager to serve me a hasty dinner and then wishing me goodnight, retire for the night to their quarters which, were in outhouses at a little distance from the guest house. I do not think that they guessed the real reason for my sojourn there and I did not enlighten them. Only once did I ask one of the bearers if the suite I was staying in, was one of the less frequented ones. He looked at me with a startled look and after stuttering for a bit, protested that no, it was very busy. In fact, all the rooms were popular with guests. By the time he had finished explaining the situation, he looked quite ashen. I did not press on. After all, he had a job to do. But I think the place had taken a toll on those who worked there. They were silent, nervous. Somewhat unhappy. I wonder what they had seen and heard there, in that house, built near an old mazaar.

Then there's the story about that corner house on South End Road, facing Lodhi Gardens. It's a two-storeyed house with an unlived in air. An early morning walker at Lodhi, told me this tale. 'That house is occupied by an MP now. But that's only for now. The spirit who lives there will see to that. He does not allow anybody to settle down. Many people have seen him. He comes out every day at dawn, takes a turn around the tombs and disappears into the mist. He wants that place for himself.' It's true that for a house that's supposedly occupied, it looks bleak and deserted, even in the afternoon sun.

As for the well-known VIP houses which carry a curse or a story on their heads – it's a fact that a certain lady politician was once advised to move from her Janpath residence, because it seemed to bring her only bad luck. The wife of a previous prime minister warned her about how ill it had been for her family. People who knew, said that an old mazaar lay in the compound. I myself have felt the vibrations which emanate from a very old peepul tree in the compound, near the bungalow. It talks of peace which never comes in Delhi, in life or in death. Those who lie there under the earth smile at human ambitions and vow that they will never let others have, what they themselves can no longer taste. This lady politician often stands under the tree or near it, when the sun is hot, and talks to visitors. She seems very attached to the house. Maybe it is too late now and the house will not allow her to move. Like the tree, it has spread out its many roots.

And so it goes on in Delhi. Amid the power and the pomp, the greed and the treachery, the intrigue and the lust, the restless dead continue to haunt the places they once knew. Are they angry? It would seem so. But they will eventually get what they want. In one way or the other. They always have. And they can afford to wait.

Jani's Morning

Shama Futehally

The mug was greeny-blue, the colour of magic. Every morning it showed another mug shining in the mirror. They were both full of delicious things. And every morning the mug was waiting for Jani. Because he had to wash everything. The yellow toothbrush, the blue toothbrush, Baba's funny stick and the other soft black brushy thing. He was reaching for it now, on tip-toe, stretched till it seemed he might suddenly coil backwards. In his woolly pyjamas his bottom stuck out like that of a little fat duck. Stretch ... stretch ... the taut finger wagged from side to side. All at once the finger hit the mug, it toppled and crashed into the basin.

There! Now he would start. He was tugging at the tap, and the knobbly steel hurt his fingers. He pulled and pulled. At once the tap gave way and there it came, exactly the same straight gleaming line. (Jani was always a little afraid that the gleaming line would be different.) He put four fingers in the water and waited for them to curl back all by themselves. He did it again. Then he moved his hand around in the water to feel the funny tingling in different parts.

Jani picked up the yellow toothbrush, held it under the water, and put it carefully in the soap dish. When he began to wash the small blue brush a miracle happened.

"Jani!" Amma called from her room. "Put the paste on my brush and I'll come and brush my teeth with you."

Jani felt as if someone had given him an ice-cream for no reason. He hadn't said it. He hadn't cried or tugged at her dressing-gown. She said it all by herself. They would stand in their special place under the golden globe, and up and down, up and down, together they would produce the white foam. They would have a tooth-brushing race. When he wasn't looking, Amma would tickle him. O what a tussle there would be! He laid the brush in the dish. He would be ready, ready, ready.

A little later Amma came in. Now she seemed a little different. Her hair was already combed. "Oh Jani!" she said. "What are you doing?"

In the way that always happened with grown-ups, suddenly everything was different. Amma was putting everything back into the mug and from the way she was doing it Jani knew there would be no race. His lips began to feel soft and trembly. Now Amma was squeezing her own paste! And grief rushed at Jani like a slap. It rushed around inside his chest, swelling it up. His eyes closed tight, and a howl emerged from Jani.

Amma stopped squeezing and looked at him with set lips. Jani couldn't stop the howl, it kept coming and coming like an endless puffy train. "Stop yowling!" Baba shouted from the room. They were both "like that" today. But Jani's chest was full of sobs, round red gulpy ones. Because that was the best part of all. To squeeze Amma's green paste, to hold the tube tightly in both hands till his very last bit of breath was gone. And then the slow beautiful reward crawled out, a green snail of paste all made by Jani. With intense care he would drape it on the brush.

"I'll do it! I'll do it!" Jani was shrieking through his sobs.

Resignedly Amma gave him the toothpaste and brush. Still gulping he began to squeeze. But he couldn't, not while Amma watched with her tight face. "Hurry up!" she said. And the train of howls began to rush out of Jani's chest once more.

Then Amma changed. Her two large arms in their woollen sleeves came round him. The tiny woollen hairs on her dressing-gown were tickling his face. "There," she said. But Jani was never going to smile again. Amma gave him a peck on the nose. Never, never. Then Amma became properly herself. She drew her arms tighter, screwed up her mouth, and gave him a long, chewy, noisy kiss on the cheek. And Jani looked up with a small smile of forgiveness.

Now they were in the room, and Jani's shirt was over his head. His little shoulder-blades stuck out like wings. His arms couldn't find the right holes. Round and round he went, like a trussed chicken. Amma and Baba were both being best. They didn't tell him to hurry. They didn't say you'll learn when you're bigger.

They stood by him, shouting nice things. "Push just a little." "Photo! Everyone smile for the photo!" Suddenly – shoosh! His arms slid through. Cheeks flushed, eyes shining, the face of a hero emerged. Amma and Baba began to clap, just as you do for babies like Munni. But Jani knew they wanted to please him so he clapped too. At once he stopped and shot a glance at Baba. "I want the story about the hairy bear," he said. Jani could seize an opportunity as well as anybody.

~

"Then," said Bai, "the lion said, "What! Another lion! And he jumped into the well."

"Then," breathed Jani.

"The ...e ... e ... n ..."

"No no!" shouted Jani. "He didn't die."

"Of course not," said Bai at once. "Then he climbed out of the well and went home and lived happily ever after."

Jani breathed a long sigh of pure happiness. Nobody told a story like Bai did. Amma couldn't roar properly – she just made a little no-good sound – and Baba didn't care whether the lion climbed out or not. He was gazing at Bai as if he would burst. Then he didn't know what to do so he jumped up with a shriek and jumped again and fell down in the grass. He lay there with little things tickling his neck, and the funny light feeling of the sun on his face.

They were on the grass beside the garden tap. It was Jani's favourite place, where he always hid when he played I-Spy with

Bai. Under the tap there was a little brown shining puddle with yellow leaves. And next to it grew a small stiff bush with purple flowers. Without warning Bai plucked a flower and stuck it behind his ear. "Girl! Girl!" she shouted, running away.

"You girl," said Jani, puffing after her. "You girl."

When she reached the swing Bai waited for him with her arms wide open. He ran straight at her and buried his head in her frock.

Bai had a different kind of smell. She was usually in the same frock, white and green with a beautiful tear at just the right place under the arms. And Bai wore a purple sweater right through the cold and now she was still wearing it even though it was so hot. Her hair was very oily and was tied back in the thick plait. Her dark skin shone like her eyes.

"What do you want to do now, Jani?" asked Bai tenderly. "Do you want to sit on the swing?"

Yes Jani wanted to sit on the swing. But it was very hot. Slowly, secretly, he was thinking what it would be like to be drinking lime juice.

Jani loved juice and he always wanted Bai to have some too. But when Ayah made his juice she never gave Bai any. When Amma gave him biscuits she always said, "Give one to Bai." You must always share, said Amma. But once when he said to Amma, "Some juice for Bai?" she didn't answer and Bai only laughed. "The juice is all for you, Jani," she said.

Now Bai was setting him on the swing. "I'll bring your juice from the kitchen," she said practically. "Would you like to come to my house and drink it?"

Oh yes. Jani loved Bai's house. It was in the little lane behind their own house and it was dark and cool with beautiful blue walls. On one wall there hung lots of shiny coloured pictures together, looking like an enormous flower. Underneath there was a little orange light. Jani thought it was the most beautiful thing he had ever seen. And he had never forgotten the time when he ran away to Bai's house very early one morning. It was like a haven of cosiness. All over the floor there were long parcels covered in quilts. Then Bai's brother's head emerged from one. Her father's from another. You never knew whose head was going to appear next.

Clutching Bai's dress with one hand, holding his mug of juice in the other, Jani stepped importantly into Bai's house. He knew what kind of a welcome he was going to get. Bai's uncle raised himself on one arm. "Well, Jani Babu!" he said. "You forgot us yesterday." Bai's uncle lived on a string bed in a corner of the house. Bai's mother looked up and smiled. She was pumping the stove. That was another thing. In Bai's house there was a beautiful round golden stove right in the middle of the floor. Now it was squeaking ... *deechoo* ... *deechoo* ... *deechoo* ... Jani held his breath. It would come. *Dhoosh*! With a thud a flaming blue circle leapt up around it. It was thudding and thudding, as if it wanted to catch him. Jani could never see it often enough. It was like the time when Baba took him to see the aeroplane and he saw it tear down the road in a frenzy and without warning enter the sky.

The flame was shouting away. On his small mat in the corner Jani felt very safe. "Will you have a *chapati*, Jani?" said Bai's mother.

"Yes one *chapati* for me," said Jani. "Just a small one" – he remembered his manners just in time. And Bai's mother rolled him a special baby *chapati* and put it on the stove.

It was also different and nice, sitting on the mat, eating *chapatis* in the middle of the floor. Something began to fill up inside him. He looked shyly at Bai. Bai looked back at him, eyes shining. When they were in her own house, Bai never talked much. She just kept looking first at him and then at her uncle or mother, as if she were proud of something.

"The *chapati* is very hot, Jani," Bai said for something to say. And Jani gravely blew a huge breath on it.

While eating he was looking at his favourite picture. "What is in that picture?" he asked Bai's mother. He knew the answer.

"That is God, Jani," she said in a different voice. "Fold your hands and do *pranaam*."

Jani had put down his *chapati* and was ready. Feeling very serious, as he did when he was being a very good boy, he folded his hands and bent his head. God was a pink man with lots of hair, who was sitting in a blue sea and appeared to be enjoying himself. Amma had told him that God lived in the sky, and Jani always spared a glance or two for Him when he left Bai's house.

"Jani is a good boy," said Bai's uncle, when Jani finally peeped. "And how old are you, Jani?"

"Two-and-a-half," said Jani carefully.

"So much! And when is your happy-birthday?"

"Soon."

"And whom will you ask?"

"I will ask Bai and Bai's Amma and you. And Amma and Baba and Munni."

They roared with laughter, as they always did. Sometime Jani would find out why. When he thought of his birthday, he imagined them all sitting on the floor at home and eating cake, just as they were eating *chapatis* here. But right now he wanted to roar with laughter and beat his knee like Bai's uncle. Amid the beating and the laughter came an important message for Jani.

"Lunch-time, Jani," Ayah was standing in the doorway. "Come along."

Jani stopped beating his knee and jumped at Ayah. "Bye-bye!" he shouted to Bai's house.

"Will you eat all your curds today?" Ayah called to his back.

"All!" Jani was halfway down the lane. "All!" he raced into the house. "All-all!" down the passage. "All-all-all-all-all-all-all-all!" round and round the table. He had become a plane.

Omens, Sacred and Profane

Namita Gokhale

Vatsala Vidyarathi was a literary lady. She had eyes like almonds, and a double helix drawn with black eyeliner stabbed her forehead. She had a vaguely Egyptian look, and favoured the South American writers, although she feared they were becoming passe. She despised alliteration, colour coordinates, synthetic gold *zari*, Dubai expatriates, and Gulshan Kumar's *bhajans*.

Vatsala worked with an advertising agency. She had done a stint in Bombay before settling down in Delhi, where, alas, the scene was not 'professional'. She had faced heartbreak thrice, twice in Bombay, and once in Hissar, where she had lost her heart to a dairy-farmer. Vatsala had gone to Hissar to get the feel of the place for a new account. The dairy-farmer was a consultant to a new Indo-Danish collaboration, and she had succumbed to his manly charms amidst the mooing of cows and malodorous whiffs of manure.

But nothing came of it. Back in Delhi, life continued as before. It took half an hour in a sputtering auto-rickshaw to get to her office in Connaught Place, sometimes even forty-five minutes. She retraced the same route across the Ring Road in the evening, through the dull Delhi dusk. She had sold her olive-green Maruti 800, bought on a Citibank loan, after a rogue tempo had run amok and repeatedly rammed into its defenceless body as it stood parked outside her ground floor Vasant Kunj flat.

The flat was pleasingly done up in muted shades and natural fabrics. Vatsala had a small study, where the pixels on her monitor flickered into the late hours of the night. 'Thus shone the lonely light in Milton's tower,' she murmured to herself, as she laboured away at the verse-drama in eighty-four stanzas with which she hoped some day to stagger the world.

She then retired to her quiet air-conditioned bedroom, where photographs of her nieces and nephews hung next to the bathroom door, and a poster for a bull-fight which she had picked up during a holiday in Spain was pasted to the wall above her bed.

The guest room, done up in anaemic pastels, was reserved for her family. When Vatsala's parents came down from Dehra Dun, she felt a bit cramped, but dutifully put up with everything, even the familiar programmed remonstrations about finding herself a nice boy soon.

At the age of thirty-five, when her firm conical breasts had mysteriously enlarged from 34B to 36, Vatsala Vidyarthi suffered a spiritual crisis. It began with a nagging question. 'To what purpose?' Vatsala would ask herself, as she gazed sorrowfully at her bowl of muesli in the mellow Delhi morning. 'To what purpose?' she would ponder, as the auto-rickshaw raced through the traffic, past the outstretched hands of beggars and babies-in-arms, through the familiar tired tenements of our country's capital, until the gracious arches of Lutyens' folly welcomed her back to work.

'Whatever for?' she would ask aloud, as she scanned the agonisingly cute copy for yet another brand of baby food. As she left office in the evenings, the mandatory black coffee still bitter in her mouth, she would resolve to find a good chartered bus that suited her timings. Then again the tired traffic, snaking across the congested arteries of the Ring Road until the Qutub Minar, lit by powerful strobes, its phallic lines cutting across the comatose sky, shook her back to the immediate concerns of existence.

Which were: fresh bread and eggs, lonely nights, power cuts, the search for a good *dhobi*, and the subconscious reaching out for another presence as she held her pillow through the long lonely night.

You might exclaim that this is merely common or sparrow angst, the city-dweller's ennui. Those of you with a humbler vocabulary may even bluntly call it loneliness, or ascribe it, in the fashion of the times, to the ever-worsening pollution in our cities. But no, Vatsala knew there was more to it, she was searching for something, and having worked in Bombay and priding herself on being a professional, she knew she would not rest until she had found it.

Now Vatasla Vidyarthi was a literal lady. To search, as in to quest, to seek, to look, to find, became a pitiless exercise in self-discipline and logistics. She took up yoga, and woke at dawn to contort herself mercilessly into a million pretzels before setting out for her office. She joined a pottery class in Garhi village, taking time off from the agency to shape damp clay into function and meaning. She took up good works; registering with an NGO to counsel late-night suicide calls. But no one called, and she had the sensitivity to see that her pottery was ungainly, and the yoga made her irritable and exacerbated her sinus.

The agency experienced a mild upheaval when her boss left, along with four colleagues, to start an advertising firm of his own. He was replaced, so swiftly that it might have been providential, by a live-wire Madrasi with a thing about the rural market. Mr Raman, 'Manny' to this friends, was a hyperactive, hyperbolic wog with an unerring ear for punch lines. Before she knew what was happening, Vatasla was packed off to the Kumbh Mela, (about which she later wrote a piece for A & M). New accounts were pouring in, and Manny instructed everyone in the agency to subscribe to at least one vernacular newspaper or magazine, in the language of their choice, to keep in touch with the masses.

Vatsala's odyssey to the real India began to tell on her copy. She wowed one and all with her artful espousal for Dunkel (sponsored by a progressive multinational) on behalf of DRAG, which, as everyone knows, is the Directorate for Research on Agriculture. A simple smudge of *kumkum* replaced the ornate artwork of the double helix *bindi*, and she regretfully bid adieu to salads after the rural E Coli bacillus had played havoc with her digestion. She decided that nail varnish did not let her toe-nails breathe, and even contemplated letting her 36B breasts out of the unnatural restraint of an underwired bra. But that would be rash, keeping in mind the turbulent daily auto-rickshaw rides through Delhi's pot-holed streets, and she decided regretfully to settle for a colourful *ghagra-choli* on weekends.

Vatsala Vidyarthi was an Indian lady, and when she was dispatched to Rishikesh to background a new account that Manny was gunning for, she went with a distinct sense of piety and reverence.

The product was a dual-purpose herbal incense-cum-mosquito mat, to be christened after the holiest river in India. The Ganges, which had already endorsed products as diverse as soap and mineral water, remained for her the river of her childhood *samskaras*. After stopping for a night with her parents in Dehra Dun (her mother was down with a flu, her father had spondilitis again), she left the next afternoon by taxi for the Ganges Riverside Retreat, which, she had been assured, was a most suitable hostelry for a single unescorted lady.

Two things happened to Vatsala in Rishikesh. She found a man, and quite coincidentally, herself. Unrepelled by the mosquito mats of solitude and sadness with which she had surrounded herself, propelled as it were, by pheromones, he came into her life.

He was a Slav, and although he was dressed all in saffron, he had the acrid manly smell of tobacco and sweat and meat-eating flesh. He strolled into her room quite by accident, mistaking it for his own. Vatsala had dutifully checked the safety-latch before settling down for the night, but of course it didn't work.

She welcomed him in as an old friend. There was something disarming about the set of his eyes and the surprising purity of his face. He wore heavy mountaineering boots, and a string of prayer beads hung around his neck. In his sturdy orange robes, he looked like a Buddhist monk returning from his travels.

They sat down together in the small balcony that overlooked the river, and listened peaceably as the steady sound of the water punctuated the silence of the night. They might have been friends forever, so instant and complete was the understanding between them.

A cold mist rose like a wraith from the river, enveloping them in odd intimacy. The stranger took out a cheroot from his voluminous rucksack. When the match burst into flame the tranquil contours of his face lit up for a brief second, and Vatasla longed to reach out and touch him.

'We cannot isolate mind from matter, nor separate the soul from the body,' he said, in a pleasantly accented voice, as he stripped off her night-shirt with clinical precision, and got to work with fanatical passion upon her body. Vatsala was so startled that she didn't protest at all, but gave herself up to the moment with feelings that bordered on detachment, if not resignation. The holy river, the early-winter mist, the smoke from his cheroot that seemed to have penetrated her every crevice; she felt as though she were floating out of herself, escaping the confines of skin and nail and shampoo into a world of extraordinary immediacy. They sported together late into the night, until the stranger shuddered to a climax somewhere deep within her, and no, it was not as it had been with the married man or the dairy-farmer.

'Now I am seeing for the first time, seeing directly without the intervention of mortal eyes', Vatsala said, only half to herself.

'I am him and he is me, we are in the river and the river is within us. There is a cosmic connectedness in it all. We are Yin and Yang, egg and yolk, Shiva and Shakti. I can, here in Rishikesh, transcend the barriers of time and space. Vasant Kunj was a dream, and the auto-rickshaw drivers, a nightmare. And even if this passion with a strange man is a sin, I can, after all, wash it all off in the Ganges tomorrow!'

The next morning she awoke with a bodyache. She was alone, naked in her bed in the hotel room, without so much as a coverlet over her. The stranger, if he had come at all, had disappeared without a trace.

Vatsala put on some clothes and phoned room service for a cup of tea. The squat Garhwali waiter hung around stubbornly for a tip. It was when she looked into her purse that she realised that she had been robbed. No wallet, no watch, no money, not even any change. Even the credit card had gone. She scrambled around, willing it to be an absurd mistake, rummaging through the dirty clothes she had thrown into the cupboard.

The waiter shrugged insolently and left. The tea turned cold. Vatsala watched as a fly settled on the skin which had formed over the tea. It drowned before her eyes.

She did not know quite how she could explain her predicament to the hotel, or to the police. Wearily, she decided to phone Manny at the agency. He would know what to do.

She couldn't get through to the operator. Vatsala sleep-walked to the front desk, where she was sure the receptionist, who was covered in layers of artificial diamonds, gave her a knowing look. Summoning up all her self-possession, Vatsala gave her the number of the agency. She ordered another cup of tea for herself and waited for the call in the small deck that overlooked the sparkling waters of the river. A flight of steps led down to a private bathing area. Ancient, decomposing garlands of marigolds floundered around the black rocks.

The receptionist informed her that the line to Delhi was down. 'After all, this is UP,' she said consolingly. Vatsala felt so lost and alone that even this note of minor sympathy was enough to breach her defences. She found herself telling the receptionist that her wallet had been stolen.

'So why don't you call the police?' the receptionist asked, scratching her underarms as she spoke. Her cream coloured blouse was circled with lines of brown sweat. Vatsala realised anew that she was well and truly marooned.

'Actually, there was hardly any money in it,' she said hastily, but she was an ineffectual liar, and the receptionist arched her finely-pencilled eyebrow in a manner that could have signified anything from scepticism to boredom. Vatsala affected an air of brave unconcern. 'I'm not the sort of person who bothers about money. The police can be such a bore,' she said, wishing, not for the first time, that she was better at untruths.

Since she wasn't sure about when she would be able to contact Manny or the agency, she decided to get down to work anyway.

She resolved to walk so as to save money, and set off on foot towards the town.

Her brief was to scout for locations for Manny's new obsession, the Ganges Herbal range of incense-coated mosquito repellents. 'It's penetration we're looking for,' Manny had said, for the umpteenth time. 'The sex is in the volume. I want you to look around, soak in the atmospherics. We're marketing a concept along with a utility. It's important to understand the mindset of the base customer. Remember, he may be illiterate, but he's no fool.'

Armed with these wise axioms and dutifully equipped with a camera and a notepad. Vatsala set off. The town appeared dirty, and not particularly holy. The river seemed tantalisingly close. It could be glimpsed, glistening like a golden ribbon, through the shanty-shops and diesel trucks that lined the road.

Vatsala was tired, her head ached and her feet hurt. The dust tickled her sinus. She retraced her way to the Ganges Riverside Retreat and ordered herself a taxi. 'Put it on my bill,' she said with as much authority as she could muster.

It was a new diesel Ambassador. It worked. The driver was polite and courteous. When they hadn't run over man or dog by the time they reached Muni-ki-Reti, Vatasla decided that her luck must have changed.

'There is an air of eternity, even timelessness, to this place,' she noted mentally, when she saw the river again. But Vatsala detested cliches. Reproaching herself for visual laziness and a dependence on preconceptions, she set about re-examining the scene. The sunlight glinted joyously on the waters. There was a silence in the air, a stillness, which was quite removed from the clatter of horns or the barking and squealing of street dogs. The water was cleaner than she had imagined it would be. A sense of gladness descended over her like a benediction. 'Who am I?' she asked herself, 'and to what purpose?' but the old question stood shorn of tension and ambiguity. She even suspected that someone, somewhere, might know the answer.

A sadhu in a saffron loincloth was observing her intently. He was muscular and sinewy and his eyes were hard and observant. She felt herself blush under his gaze, and hurried on. Small children, bleached urchins with the sun in their eyes, sold her little polythene packs of fish feed. They ran away clutching the money she gave them, the sounds of their laughter only adding to the silence.

She was giddy with the sun and the heat and a strange, unfamiliar sense of elation. A ferry-boat slithered up right in front of her, and before she knew it she had purchased a ticket, and was halfway across the water.

The boat was full of people, people in polyester shirts and synthetic *zari*-bordered saris, the great Indian masses. She looked at them curiously, searching for signs of communality. 'Not that I feel superior,' she told herself hastily, 'it's just that our backgrounds are so different.'

The woman to her right, her face covered with a *ghungat*, threw some pellets of fish-feed into the river. Huge fish crowded by the prow of the boat, greedily gobbling up the brown pellets before they dissolved in the muddy water. They looked fat and grubby, obese and dissolute. 'They feed on flesh,' the woman on her right said shyly to no one in particular.

A rush of river-air hit Vatsala in the face; it was an exhilarating bouquet of fish-pong and iodine. She felt complete, liberated from her skin, forgetful of her many failures and recent humiliation. 'Is this an epiphany?' she wondered aloud, then reproached herself for being too dissective.

Across the river the atmosphere was quite different, more charged. Everything, from the ambling cows to the brass amulets piled up for sale by the riverbank, reeked of the sacred.

Vatsala Vidyarthi was a hard-working lady. She sat down by the steps of the bathing ghat and meticulously set about noting and tabulating her impressions. But the steep winding road, the *pamnam chadars*, the fragrance of marigolds: these images moved her to poetry and she decided to pen a free style haiku instead:

The river flows
on and on
even as the flowers
are caught in the eddies

Then decided it was not very original.

By now she was feeling very hungry. The distinctive aroma of *parathas* frying on the griddle, bathed in real *ghee* (a smell she normally despised), lured her up a narrow lane. A fat man, fatter than a circus lady, dressed as a Bhahurupiya, simpered invitingly at his customers. A sign behind him proclaimed 'The one and only Chotiwala! Please try for taste.'

The idea came to her in the conventional shape of a bulb, a thousand watt bulb. This was the perfect setting for their product. It would zap the rural psyche. It was endorsing Ganges Herbal incense mosquito-mats! It was original, it was authentic, it was humorous. It would give Manny a real rush.

Vatsala ordered herself a full meal, and gorged herself on *alloo* and *puri* and *raitha* rather as the grubby fish in the Ganges had done. 'They feed on flesh,' she said to herself reflectively. At the next table, a silent South Indian family was pensively contemplating a plate of vegetarian chow mein. When Vatsala realised that she had no money, she looked around her widely, wondering what to do. The establishment did not look inclined to credit. Perhaps the South Indian family might lend her some cash.

A male presence settled itself on the chair across hers. The acrid smell of marijuna clung to him like a blanket. He smiled at her from deep within his Slavic eyes, and companiably offered her a drag. Vatsala looked at him with shock and horror and revulsion. When he touched her a shiver rippled through her body. Fighting back her tears, she rushed out, weaving her way through the crowded tables until she was finally on the narrow lane outside. Something would not let her go and she found herself turning back, searching through the squeeze of customers. A sweaty waiter was handing him her bill, along with a steel bowl containing a residue of aniseed and sugar. He took out his wallet and paid up with good grace, counting out the money in crisp new notes. An amused smile lit up his tranquil features. He was a detestable villain.

'At least the bastard paid for the meal,' Vatsala muttered to herself, wiping her eyes with the corner of her *chunni*. In the right light, the episode could even be viewed as funny. In fact, it was hilarious. She would tell Manny about it, and he would realise that she was not just a blue-stocking, that she could be quite daring when she so chose.

When she returned to the riverside resort there was another young woman, also draped in artificial diamonds, stationed at the reception. She handed the room keys to Vatsala with an elegant sigh, then resumed the thoughtful scrutiny of her scarlet finger nails.

The room had been freshly sprayed with a powerful and malodorous insecticide. Hordes of delicate moths lay shuddering in their death throes by the balcony. The sharp smell of the chemicals assaulted her larynx. 'What they need is some Ganges Herbal incense mosquito-mats,' she said to herself, quite loudly this time. It was becoming a habit.

She looked down at the Ganges. It looked no different from yesterday, the same damp river-mist, the lapping waters by the shore, the steady rhythm of the mainstream. Across the river a rectangular line of fire lit up the sparse forest cover. A corpse was burning merrily.

'And we are here as on a darkling plain,
swept with confused alarms of struggle and flight,
where ignorant armies clash by night.'

Vatsala recited dreamily. For some reason, Matthew Arnold

seemed particularly appropriate for the time and moment. The phone rang. It was Rita, the girl from the reception. 'We met in the morning,' she said. 'I have to speak to you.' It sounded serious.

She arrived at the door so quickly that Vatsala concluded that she must have telephoned from the next room. She was clutching her handbag, and fingering her fake diamond necklace with her shell-pink extremities. She was so excited that she practically fell into the room. 'I've recovered the money,' she said, emptying four thousand rupees in cash, two gold bangles and a credit card on to the double bed that straddled the room. 'It was the waiter! I don't know how he managed to get in! Perhaps you forgot to lock the door or you'd gone for a bath."

Vatsala remembered that she had been quite naked when she awoke, without even the benefit of a coverlet. She blushed, and stuttered her thanks.

'The management has already fired him,' the voluble Rita continued. 'I always suspected that there was something wrong with him. I'm very intuitive, you know. I think you'd agree that we needn't call the police.'

Vatsala wondered what his name had been, and if she would ever find out, now. He had made love to her, and he had paid for her lunch. Vatsala Vidyarthi was a lady, and she wondered at her own behaviour.

'I think I'll return to Delhi now,' she said faintly. Before she knew it she had paid the bill, and was bundled into an Ambassador car, a ramshackle one this time. She debated about whether to stop over at Dehra Dun and visit her parents, but she decided against it.

Vatsala Vidyarthi was a real lady, and decided to keep the incident to herself. Whenever she remembered it she felt a deep sense of regret, followed by an inordinate relief. Sometimes she would sigh when she scanned a page of particularly tedious copy, or penned a haiku, or read a poem by Matthew Arnold.

'Perhaps,' she would think – 'who knows!'

A short story is supposed to snap shut at the end with a sort of satisfactory click, but it would be difficult to distort this tale to fit such an artistic purpose.

My quarrel with the short story is precisely that it imposes a false order and symmetry on events, forcing impressionable young minds to anticipate a similar state from the inchoate mess that is generally life.

Even Mr Raman (Manny to his friends) agreed in the course of an abstract discussion that a punch line is not always essential to a good denouement.

Cry, My Beloved Child

Vandana Kumari Jena

It's raining. I love rain. I love making paper boats and floating them on open drains. I love getting drenched and swinging my wet hair from side to side as the water dribbles down my back. I love the smell of the mud, the richness and the fragrance of the rain-washed earth. The cry of the peacock as it breaks into a dance. So different from a baby's cry.

As if on cue, you start crying. Your face puckers up. Tiny, red-faced, like a little Hiawatha. Your hands balled into little fists. Eyes charcoal black. Not mine. Mine are hazel, flecked with gold. Then whose? I do not know. I will never know.

But you are flesh of my flesh. Blood of my blood. Eyes puckered, as if shielding themselves from the harsh glare of the world. The nurse has come. I know what she will say. "Lift up your blouse. Feed the baby." Feed you? Allow you to drain me completely? To sap my energy, and leave me exhausted, an empty shell of what I once was? For three days, I have stood the pain. I can't bear it any more.

"Sister, I can't feed him, take him away from me," I say. But no sound emanates. I can hear my silent pleas. But they can't. Am I dumb? Or is everyone here deaf?

The face of Sister Nivedita intrudes. "Lift the child," she says, persuasively, and my hands move to pick you up. "Feed it," she commands and instinctively, I obey. Nivedita. The name sounds familiar. Namita. Nivedita. Nivedita. Namita.

What do names matter anyway? For me, everything is a haze, a blur. Sometimes, I think I am losing my mind. My past – that is a slate, wiped clean. There is a medical name for it, my condition. I forget what it is.

"It's a trauma. It has resulted in loss of speech," the doctor said. Perhaps.

Sister Nivedita is here. She asks me eagerly, "Do you remember?"

~

"Remember me till I'm dead ... Oranges and lemons, sold for a penny ..." A picture swims before me, wearing a blue pinafore and a white blouse, hair tied up in pigtails, jumping around the playground. What school was it? The name eludes me. But it was just down the road. It was lined with 'gulmohar' trees, whose crimson flowers in full bloom always reminded me of a forest fire.

And my house, it had a name. Yes, it is coming back to me. I have a name too. And a big white house with a courtyard. Where Ma sliced up slivers of mangoes and put them out into the courtyard to dry, filling up the entire house with the aroma of raw mangoes. Where large bottles of 'aam ka achar' were then kept in the sun till the raw green skin turned a deep yellow which melted on your tongue. Where I would steal the 'achar' and eat dollops of it along with a crisp, six-layered 'paratha' straight from the 'tawa'.

Yes, it exists. You, my dear child, will no longer be homeless. When I get out of this place, this sanatorium, or whatever they call it, you and I will go look for our house. We'll trudge along, with you nestling in the crook of my arms while we search for our house. And Ma will be so happy when I get back. For years, she and I were the only ones after father died.

You and I, my little one, share a similar destiny. I never saw my father. He died in an accident before I was born. And you will never know yours. But there is a difference. My father's photograph hung from the drawing room wall. And, as Ma and I made garlands to hang around his photograph, I could feel him smiling benevolently at me. But you?

But wait, there is something wrong. There will be no Ma at the gate. I last saw her covered in a white sheet, as the neighbours whispered, "What will happen to Namita?" Me.

And then Baba's relatives took charge of me. "Come back to us," they said. And I left my home.

"Will you be able to get there on your own?" Ravi 'chacha', my neighbour, had asked, at the station.

"Of course 'chacha'," I had said, smiling through my tears.

The train was due to arrive at noon. But it broke down en route. "God knows when it will reach. I hope you have someone to receive you?" enquired a fellow passenger. I hoped so too, especially as the evening had melted into the night by the time the train arrived at the station.

But there was no familier face waiting for me at the station in this unknown city. No scooter or taxi was willing to go either, as the house was every close to the station.

Dejectedly, I started walking with my suitcase in my hand. And then, they came. They appeared to be shadows which suddenly detached themselves from the wall and assumed human – no, demonic-shapes.

They were four of them. They headed straight for me. And I, disoriented and fatigued by the journey and the sweltering heat, wondered what they wanted. They laughed. And I knew. And hoped that I would die.

But I didn't. Not when they dragged me, kicking and screaming. Not when they threw me on a sagging old cot. Not when they put their smelly, sweaty hands on my mouth to smother my screams. To choke my cries. I struggled. I fought. I kicked. I bit. And cried some more. But there was no escape.

"After every night, however dark, there is a dawn," says Sister Nivedita. But she, in her white gown, dedicated to the love of God, what does she know of life, of its todays and tomorrows? What does she know of the pain, that tearing, searing pain, which is tearing me apart? Of humiliation? Of rage? There will be no escape and there will be no rescue for there are no heroes in this world, only villains.

And I am left to die, day by day. With these white-gowned nuns who found me almost comatose and took me in. To nurse "the wonder that is growing within you," they said. Did they not understand that I loathed you, my son, all these months? Loathed the blood that mingled with mine to give birth to you? But I could not tell them – I had already drifted into a soundless world.

It was when the police came for questioning and asked me my name that I realised I had lost my voice. And my memory. "Trauma," they said. I hated it, hearing but not being heard, screaming silent screams of anguish. Not remembering my own name.

~

But now, I remember everything. My childhood, my youth. And the dark alley into which they dragged me, the cot on which they threw me on and the sweaty hands which clasped my mouth.

Like this.

The vice-like grip on my throat.

Like this.

Blotting out my cries.

Like this.

My limp, silent form.

Like this.

Sister, what is wrong? Why doesn't anyone come?

Oh, she's here. Why is she eyeing me so strangely? Why has she taken you from me? How did you get all those red weals on your throat? Why are your lips so waxen and pale?

Oh, my son! You were crying so lustily just moments ago. Why have you stopped? Why are you silent now? Cry once, just once. Cry, my beloved child, cry.

Give Me Back My Country

Manju Kak

Growing out of buttresses and arches, cutting through the cracked masonry of pigeon encrusted domes are bastard pipals taken root in the sun drenched stone of the Red Fort. They grow sometimes tall, like that one there, to shelter barbers, madmen, charlatans, and shrines. And a *paan wala* who lifts bold black eyes to stare into mine, safely distant, in my balcony. The Fort has long disembowelled dynastic power, all human life. Only the bastard trees remain. Knowing this, still I mourn?

There are many houses tucked away in my memory. They seep into my vision, layer by layer, like the trifle Reva loves. There are those in which I lie vacant nights in open spaces looking up at marigold garlands of stars, there are tiled grand galleon ones when I am contained in cotton quilts of winter warmth. Ones vaunting head dresses of stucco crosses, embroidered shields, vain *guldastas* sprouting wispy clumps of dry thicket, twirling emblems all, of kingly masonry embossed upon colonial red brick. And there is ... this. If I shut my left eye I will not see the reinforced concrete of the projecting balconies of other flats. I will see nothing but the sky and the foliage of a lone inflamed gulmohar weeping copious red tears and once more ... I will be home.

Could I have picked up the reddish roof tiles mouldy with age and used them in my new apartment? I could ... and yet, they wouldn't hold the same way because they wouldn't be in that same house down the lane behind the railway siding nor would I hear the hooting of the coal-engines drawing up at Prayag Raj station. I really can't build another house, tile by tile, can I? But I can build it on paper, word for word, and it will share the same sweet fragrance of that one, because it will again be the selfsame configuration of smells and thoughts. Except ... for one thing. The people. I have to bring the old people back, people whose smells clung to the spidery cracks of limewashed walls, smells long buried yet not banished. Yes, there will have to be smells and sights ... and weddings.

And ... Sarju Yadav. Sarju will have his strong mustachioed body lurking in the shade of the deep veranda where he will be talking to Reva of the University, of the lightning strike his Union has called. Sarju will have his motorcycle gang wearing little green flags stuck in their headbands. They will be the green gold bandits of the KBD and they will bike down Katra, block all traffic, stacatto gun shots from their bikes rallying spirits, righteous in youth, raise slogans strong with sound. Shops will crank shutters and, again, nothing will come of the day.

Sarju Yadav will drive his motorcycle upto my gate, watch Reva get off it, patiently explain why it is wrong for her to live like this. Reva will glance back and not see me watching through the wire mesh door because it will be dark inside and Reva will agree with him yet, tremblingly bolt back the fragile eggshell of understanding, culled from books and theories vaguely digested, fearful of not being able to mend the fragments it will shatter my life into. Fearful of betraying the house that has held her father's dreams and mine.

But Sarju Yadav will be strong with muscular bands about his arms. Sarju Yadav will be real. And Reva will feel him broad beside her, And, tossing back the slippery strands of her washed hair she will go with him, riding against the wind. Sarju will take his motorcycle down the road blowing his horn and the public in the bazaar will cleave aside. They feel his power, the power of the students behind him. He will topple vendors' stalls straining under fruit, cheap plasticware, fresh greens. Reva's head will half-turn, glance at the bruised goods, at the eyes of the hawker, victim once more, of the selfsame power they shout slogans against and she will wince. But she will not murmur words of rebuke that hover upon the threshold of her mind, she will say nothing because Sarju's arms will be around her and she will be flying high, exhilarated.

And the house sticky with night mist will be left mourning.

Houses have a will of their own. They grow into spaces, spilling like saucers of milk finding the slope in the floor, and when they don't want to see the worlds around them changing they slip filmy masks over their heads. Houses hold secrets. Houses wear clamps of steel that won't let those they hold within, stray. But Reva strayed when she sat on Yadav's motor cycle.

Reva had a gift to dream, a gift she had from me. I wear that mask, a membranous embryo, and in my space-ship I leave here and go where my heart will take me.

Sarju Yadav always wanted Reva from the time that he lurked in the dark shadowy veranda of my house not daring to come in. For inside he would recall the smell of tobacco from my husband's cigar, the mustiness from rich dank carpets laid in a monsoon room lit by a stream of dim yellow light from a hanging grape chandelier and the misty white streak of a ventilator ray, none bold enough to dispel gloom. He would hear a whip lash in the curling ends of my questions. Sarju Yadav's rippling muscles grow slack and limp under the glistening threads of his terricot kurta worn over light brown terylene pants split apart at the seams and flaring out ever so slightly that give them away as second-hand. They are a bit incongruous on his broad muscular frame. I smile. This man dressed so, cannot trouble my ordered world. But he steps back. He has delivered the letter that has come in my absence at the outhouse he inhabits. And he will retreat. He *must* retreat as he has always done, as his father did when he toiled in my garden. Wait, he has stopped by the gate and he is thinking. He turns, strides back with the tail of his kurta sashaying behind him, a duck's fin, his firm steps slow as they climb up. He coughs against the wire grill door. "What is it?" I ask sharply. "It's Reva, bibiji," he says. My voice turns sharper. I do not like him using her name like he was her born equal. "Reva bibi," I snap. "What of her?" His voice turns off-key, unable to toss his defiance in the sure manner he wants to.

"It's Reva," he repeats, petulant insolence lacing his voice, "who was caught in the *gherao* today." A cold coil in my stomach. Which *gherao* this time, I question myself uselessly, for I know the pattern of it all. "The Committee members bailed her out," he informs flatly. He's sent them to, I know. "Send her in when she returns," I command, chilly, my fear hissing out. But I should know better, "No, Wait. Let her come on her own."

I do not want him carrying messages. Do I see a grin on his face? How can I see his face, it's his retreating back that I see but his back is grinning, his broad chest is grinning, that thick curly crop is ... my heart misses a beat, he oils his hair till it glistens and the sweet sticky perfume of Cantharadine clings to the mesh door. "Wait," I call, shrill. He stops. He was expecting me to. "Wait, you. Yadav, was she hurt?" I do not want to ask him but the words come, laced with Bailey's Irish cream in the afternoon. He turns his head ever so slightly – will not come up to me or the house but from out there yells back.

"No."

Just no, a bald no.

I have betrayed my inner health, the sanctity of my inner life to him with evidence of my anxiety, and he has understood. My anxiety, strung a live tension wire links me with his retreating body, stretching like the Wrigley's Reva's chewed as a child. He knows, he will let it draw and then snap at will, his will.

Why did the good man keep poor students in his outhouses? He should have left them be where they belonged, but he wanted to help bring change, to do his bit as his mission school teachers had taught him, as he had felt the stirring in the cold fog of Leeds returning from classes in tropical medicine. But, just now I cannot think of him, I can only think of her, with rage. She wraps that *dupatta* about her neck and strides the University's campus shouting slogans. They put messy oily hands about her smooth arms and shoulders and smoke *bidis* passed from mate to mate. The sweet smell clings to her clothes. I made her wear a cotton voile saree and my seed pearls and how beautiful she looked standing in the whitewashed portico of our house receiving Professor Joshi and his wife and son, an engineer from IIT. They could move in here, they could have all the rooms even. I would keep the back room, lock it, then go to Brindavan. See other widows bathing at the ghat, take a room at the ashram and watch the sun, red orb, setting on the pale rippling water of the Yamuna. I could.

Is Reva hurt? Could she be? She will brush past the wrought iron gate, the metal nameplate vibrating with her motion, her soiled *khadi kurta* clinging about her slim body, her cloth bag sprouting notebooks slung carelessly upon her shoulder.

She will not look at my face, eyes puckered, anxious, brow tense. She will walk straight to the kitchen and poke about, not care for the things in the fridge but pick up the leftover *rotis* ayah has made and slopping some cold *sabzi*, roll it up and eat, hands unwashed. I will walk down the veranda into the garden, my eyes will be behind me, watching inside out, unseeing what lies in front, but visualising each step my daughter takes. I will shrivel at her dirty fingers doling cold food onto a steel *thali* but I know I cannot turn around and put a cloth on the table, lay a mat and dainty dishes. I know I cannot give her boiled water she will scorn. Too long she has stood alongside queues where women line at pumps and water comes in a trickle from a sputtering tap, watching.

She will not tell me of the arrest. And I cannot tell her I have learnt of it through Sarju Yadav. But he will ask her if I know. He will joke with her about me. He will question her about the intimate details of her life. He will smoke *bidis*, sweet, meet other mates' eyes, lashes dipping upon irises of yellowing hope, will loll on his *charpai* and she will be amongst them, and the smell of his oil will cling to her clothes.

Sarju Yadav will graduate this year. But he bathes his buffalo with the same vigour as his father did. Reva says to him, Sarju teach me, and he holds her hand under his and alongside, and gently they feel the teats. Their hands go up and down in motion. Sarju Yadav's *lungi* strides up and slips open. In modesty he stands, folds it in half and tucks it about his waist. Now he squats, the checked cloth taut against his hairy thigh. She squats too, having tied her *dupatta* across her waist. Then he holds her hand and raises himself slightly, holds the teat and presses it down. She does the same. They do it in unison. Her hands over the plump healthy flesh and his firm dark ones over hers. I can shout, I could call out. She will look defiant, and he will wear that amused look. He will finally know about us.

There are days when I lie in bed, as if asleep but sleep won't come. I strain to hear sounds from Reva's room, of her putting away pens, books, of the clatter of a pencil falling, of the soft strain of the light from her lamp, the same lamp she used to read Pinter, Chekov, medical manuals from. I dread it most when there is no rustle, when there is no light, when the lamps go off, when I cannot hear the sounds of her sleep. I dare not get up, I dare not see her bed unslept in, have small footfalls taken them away through the creeking swing door of the pantry? Fancy has paved a road for her that will take her off on an aeriel highway to his room, a room filled with laughter of raucous friends, and she will roll into the dip of his *charpai*, snuggle against him and his mates, and they will again pass arms about her shoulders; comrade, some *garam chai*, they will nudge. Come my Reva, come comrade of my night; and in the morning again I will see his face. Screams will split open my mind and I will spit on that … Sarju Yadav.

He would not dare, he would not … not when the good doctor was alive … no then the smell of his cigar had kept him obsequiously at the door, where it was decreed he should remain. Hush, hear, what is it, that … that noise building up. So early? It comes louder. Who are they? Why … it is those Yadavs and Mewas and Jhurris! Again in procession? They are stopping at my gatepost. Why are they stopping by my gatepost? Look, they are holding aloft those green flags again. They are shouting slogans … about caste, about liberty, about land … whose land? They are shouting against an old lady, living in a large sombre house full of memories, while they, youth, memories to make, live in outhouses? Their shouts grow louder, throw out the *netas*, throw out the teachers …

throw out this old ... witch ...? Is it ... I? But ... this *my* home ... is this not *my land*.

What has the good doctor done, serpents in my bosom, what did I do wrong? I kept them in my home, they used my water, my electricity ... they used my daughter ... and now ... they want to take my land too? Yooou bi...cchu Yadav. Reva, oh my Reva is she too with them? Who will tell me?

She comes running, in her outstretched hand a green banner, she comes running towards the gate, her hair streaming. She slams it, is locking it and sticking the flag upside down to bolt the gate post. They are chasing her but she is holding the bamboo post of the banner horizontally between her chest and gate. She is barring them with her frail body. They are screaming at her to let them in and she is shouting back. I cannot hear what she says but I see Sarju Yadav, taller and stronger than the lot, pushing his way to the front and begging her to move away. He is pointing a finger at me proud and distant in my porch and she is beating her chest and pleading with him. He is cursing, raising his hands threateningly, but she holds steadfast. The crowd is surging. They want to burst the gate open and trample over her, they look sullenly at Sarju Yadav. Why won't he let them, why is he arguing with this ... slip of a girl who lives in a large house and cannot choose? What use can she be to them? What power can her diminutive form hold over him? But she is standing still, she is taunting him, she is ... spitting on the ground.

I am frozen with fright, I cannot move, I want to run to her and hold her in my arms. But I know all my strength cannot hold the mob. It will come in like the deluge, it will take her and me. Wait … somehow something has stood still. I can hear only her voice, only hers … Sarju Yadav is still and so are those others. Slowly the kaleidoscope of people shift, colour, a new pattern I see … they are drifting, the people … they are melting. As they scatter away I see the last of them leave. My body defreezes, the nerves that have tensed slacken and I move very slowly towards her, but she is immobile. I walk erect and proud to the gate. Beyond, there is no one. I cannot believe a minute ago it was crowded. I move slowly and reach my daughter and I put my hand to her shoulder. She shakes it off. Slowly I place it again. I feel the tremor. I know she is crying. Ah Reva, She has … chosen.

"Come," I tell her.

"Come Reva, your tea has grown cold."

We sit in the dining room where the evening sun streams in, we see Sarju Yadav's buffalo lowing, but the outhouses are bare. Tomorrow he will take his buffalo away.

Tomorrow I will call my lawyer. He will talk to brokers. I need a new house, we need to move away from this crumbling mofussil town where the good doctor and his father practised, to a new city, a strong city where there are people on scooters and cars, where there are shopping malls and cinema halls and colleges where there are no strikes, where on Sunday evenings you can go to the club. I need to play cards again. It isn't so difficult to build a new house. I can always take my things from here, cupboards, tiles.

And Reva? … I know what my Reva wants. I know what her body longs for. It is for the warm strength of Sarju Yadav, for the muscled tensile strength of his large hands to wrap themselves about her slim body. She wants to feel their coarseness, the smell of oil in his hair, the shape of his brass *lota*, its heavy round bottomed metal in her hands. She wants to fuse her body onto his on the taut twisted hemp of his *charpai*. She wants to feel it swing below their weight. She wants it to sink, sink down as she feels one with Sarju Yadav. She wants to enter his spirit, she wants to steal some of it for herself. She wants him to be part of her, his oil, his *lota*, his hands that milch buffalo, the heady smell of stale sweat, she wants him and through him ... she wants to inherit her country.

I cannot let her have it.

Simone de Beauvoir and the Manes*

Lakshmi Kannan

Translated from the original Tamil by the Author

"Oh yes, there's no doubt about it, whatsoever. You'll definitely grow and develop like the French writer Simone de Beauvoir some day. All in the course of time."

They said the same things, almost all of them. But when Uma heard it for the fifth time, it took her well beyond the jaded surprise to the annoyance caused by the repetition. The statement now seemed to stand in front of her, where she could see the two ends of it, visibly drooping with fatigue on both sides. Also, she got a creepy feeling that the ones who made bold to say this were doing so with a glib ease. Because what they said had the ring of a well-rehearsed line.

Uma was not getting any younger. She remembered how scared

---

* **Manes:** Ancestral spirits or the spirit of a dead person regarded as an object to be venerated or appeased.

she was once, of the prospect of growing old. She was twenty-five then. She thought that old age would catch up with her one day abruptly, like some terrible disease. Only now she realised that ageing was more like a long, extended twilight that slowly, relentlessly, crawled upon you. Even now, she continued to hear the same line : 'You'll be like Simone de Beauvoir'. She heard it again and yet again like a tune from the one-stringed *ek tara.* Only different people plucked at the solitary string in different ways and made different sounds.

Uma flushed with embarrassment when she remembered her twenty-fifth year. She had written some shallow poems and some lightweight articles and she had carried them around in a basket on her head, hawking her wares in the market-place of magazines and newspapers where there was a shrill sales-pitch. She remembered all that disquietingly. Once, something she wrote had been rejected three times in the market-place, shattering that very brittle thing called an 'ego'. It was then that she had heard the reference to Simone de Beauvoir for the first time. Uma remembered how she had collapsed on a chair, thoroughly demoralised by the third rejection-slip of her writing. And Shekar had materialised in front of her, to sprinkle her back to life with refreshing rose-water.

"Really Uma, you must believe in yourself. At least believe me when I say that you'll certainly develop like Simone de Beauvoir some day. I'm sure about that."

She drank it in thirstily, and was eager for more.

"Yes indeed. Have some faith in yourself. Actually, what you need is a proper climate for your writing. And a congenial companion who understands what writing is all about. Given these conditions, your writing will bloom and flourish. You'll then see for yourself how you'll develop into yet another Simone..."

Shekar was thirty-seven. His words spilled out firm and rounded. A firmness which supported her young spine like a strong pillar. He took her hand resting on the table and held it in his: "Your writing is like you, very, very delicate. Both need to be protected."

Holding on to her hand, he had said: "All these things – a family, parents, a home, uncles, aunts, festivals, weddings – they make such a din that your writing will wither away if you allow yourself to be overwhelmed by them. Entrust yourself to the care of a suitable companion, the way Simone de Beauvoir did."

This man Shekar. He has written three full-length novels, a play and many short stories. He is already well-known. And yet he respects me, *me!* And my writing... She mused over his words. A small voice protested from a corner of her head. Fool, you can't hold a candle to Simone, it whispered. How can you be compared to Simone? Why, it's absurd, you greenhorn. You're much too young yet and have a long way to go. And you'll have to work a lot, lot more to develop into anything like Simone.

Besides, like her, you need to be creative about your own life. You'll have to dissolve yourself in life, like Simone did Experimentally? May be, but she did nevertheless. She dug up deep with courage and surfaced with some bitter truths. Look at you. Still imprisoned within the narrow confines of what you call 'beautiful poems'. Trapped within that, you're locked up in your petty little ideals, objectives. Learn to suspect yourself, learn to suspect the very ideals you've set for yourself. They just protect you from what is unknown. Break those dwarfish walls, smash them down and put your neck out into the wide world, even if it hurts. Come on!

"What are you thinking about, Uma? Do you think I'm extravagant in drawing parallels?"

Uma was stumped by his shrewd guess.

"Look Uma, let's make a pact. From now on at least, let's dedicate ourselves to writing. Totally. Don't look upon my wife or your parents as big hurdles. Let each of them stay in his/her/their own context. We'll keep them as a kind of background music. You and I are gifted to create. We'll have to distance ourselves from these mundane social roles and lead our lives independently."

Back home, Uma's mother Mangalam came down hard on her husband.

"But I told you about him a long time back, don't you remember? This boy Rajan, he comes from the family of Sundaram's father-in-law. I was told he is highly educated. Has good prospects in his profession. He is good looking too. What's more, his family looked so eager when they asked for our Uma in marriage. Why don't you clinch the matter quickly before the coming month of *Thai*?* You drag your feet so sluggishly ..."

"But Mangalam, Uma wants to complete her Ph.D. before she gets married. She also wants to go abroad on a scholarship. That's

---

*Thai: Name of the tenth Tamil month from mid January to mid February, considered very auspicious for marriage.

why..." her father could not complete his sentence,

"Ask your daughter to complete her Ph.D. after marriage. And tell her we'll allow her to go abroad only after she has had her first child," said Mangalam, firm as ever.

"Oh Mangalam, then everything will get so complicated for the poor girl," the father remonstrated with her.

"I know what's best for her. We can't afford to go lax. On Uma rests the continuity of a whole generation of our family. Moreover, a lively, educated girl needs to be protected even more than a girl who stays at home. Don't you know this simple truth, as a father? You've no wisdom, none whatever."

Familiar noises. Now they reached Uma with a fading exigency. Was Shekar right after all, about the way things fall back as some kind of a background music when one withdraws? A music that is mild, even dispensable? From now on, let me live for my writing alone, thought Uma...

"Uma, life is short, very short indeed. Don't waste your time," said Shekar, his voice low as he bent forward to hold her hand in his. She did not pull her hand away.

"No I won't," she had nodded, earnestly. "I promise I'll never waste my time."

She imagined herself writing copiously on sheet after sheet of paper. They fluttered and flew around her. She stayed awake for long hours in the night and wrote furiously. She dreamed that she toured all around the country and met people from different walks of life. The name 'Uma' was splashed in every newspaper and magazine. She saw her name shining luminously. She was determined to write more and more, and bring out full-length books one by one, just like this Shekar here...

~

Back home from work, Uma hardly had the time to eat her meals or rest. She could not sit down to write, or even spend some quiet moments thinking about what to write. For as soon as she reached home, the telephone would ring. Incessantly. At the other end of the wire, Shekar's voice was snappy, crackling with annoyance:

"Where on earth have you been? When can we meet? I never find you in the university.

"Where do you hide yourself?"

Eventually, Shekar resorted to hijacking her on the way home from work.

"It's been a long time since we met. You're always in a great hurry to go home, saying your father will be angry if you're late. Hell, what a life."

"Shekar, I'm working on a book. I've been busy..."

"Oh, shut up. Come on, let's get out of this damn place. Tell you what. I'm going to Jammu next month on work. Join me there and we'll go up to Kashmir. I'll book a cottage for the two of us in Pahalgam."

"Shekar! Really, you've impossible ideas. I can't do that. Besides, I've just started writing something and how can you, of all the people, ask me to drop this work and ..."

"Ha! Composing a great epic, are you? Tell me frankly once and for all. What's more important for you? Me or your silly scribblings?"

Uma was speechless with shock. She turned and left for home.

Simone, Simone, Simone. And Sartre, Sartre, Sartre. Why did I allow myself to be led on to build dreams around this couple and us? Why did I nurse notions about them when I know next to nothing about either of them, when 1 haven't even bothered to read about their lives. I just went along with whatever Shekar said, and today my half-baked knowledge is responsible for this impasse. I can only blame myself for that...

For the next few weeks, something egged her on to hunt for materials regarding Simone de Beauvoir and Jean-Paul Sartre. From various libraries, Uma gathered all that she could lay her hands on – their works, critical works on their books, their lives, their memoirs, their articles, interviews and autobiographical excerpts. Gripped by an enormous hunger to devour the details and facts culled from the books, she immersed herself in their lives, ignoring the telephone which continued to ring maddeningly. Her parents exchanged curious glances, and the phone rang out hysterically in the silence of the living room.

"Uma, why do you pore over books all day and night. You'll ruin your eyes. Just look at your face, it's looking so tired. You don't have to do research like this, at the cost of your health," said Mangalam.

"Your mother is right. Be more outgoing, meet your friends, enjoy yourself. You're too young to be cooped up indoors all day with books," said her father.

Uma absorbed what her parents said. Just like she absorbed

every single detail about Simone and Sartre culled from books and old journals. In 1929 Simone shone as a star-student of Philosophy at the University of Sorbonne in France. Sartre was in the same department. Steadily, the two of them always held on to the top positions in their classes and evolved as fine, articulate intellectuals.

How Simone and Sartre got acquainted with each other, became close friends and eventually decided to live together without the ritual of marriage, an institution they scorned; how they lived for a long time as an exemplary literary couple; how they faced the inevitable problems of opting for an unorthodox lifestyle – Uma avidly assimilated all the details. She noted some familiar paradigms that surfaced. Sartre could always count upon Simone even as he gathered many girl friends on the side. His affairs with these women were accepted in a 'wifely' manner by a stoic Simone. As a gesture of equality, Sartre suggested that Simone could have relationships too with other men if she wanted, but Simone could not/did not/would not compete with Sartre in this. She remained choosy and mature about the friends she made.

Sartre got his women easily. Some of them were 'conquests', even so he just as easily tired of them and had no hesitation in unceremoniously shaking them off to resume his writing again, undisturbed. When he felt the need for women again, he found them.

Meanwhile, Simone got very attached to the American writer Nelson Algren. She respected his work and was so happy in his company that whenever she was with him, she sensed her own womanhood blooming alive as a thing that was whole and complete. Nelson Algren. Within his embrace, she enjoyed the new freshness of her own body, the curious feeling it gave her of stepping away from herself to experience a new tangible womanhood within her being. A small universe, lovely, clean and gentle, germinated magically between them. But there came a day when even Nelson Algren burst out in exasperation: "I don't like this arrangement at all. The way you come from Paris so casually to visit me in the US, like you're on a holiday or something, to spend a couple of days, after which it's time for you to return to Paris. This is no good."

"But what can I do. Nelson? I've a house in Paris. I've my work too."

"You've your Sartre in Paris, say that. I know you go back for him, I know that only too well."

"Nelson, please,.."

"Look, I can't stand this any more. It's agonising. Sartre possesses you totally. You only throw the crumbs of life at me. You belittle me."

"How can I leave Sartre ...?"

"See, I was right in my guess, wasn't I? You go on as if you're his wedded wife. Simone, listen to me. Forget about Sartre and move over to the US. Live with me."

"Oh, but how can you suggest ...?"

"Fine then, if you don't agree to that, don't visit me like this. There's no point. Don't torture me like this. Unshackle me Simone, please."

Simone had steeled her heart and returned to Paris, resolving not to meet Algren ever again. All through her journey the questions chased her, haunted her : what urged her to continue living with Sartre? Was it a dependence, a kind of bondage, or merely a force of habit? What's the nature of this relationship? Some answers surfaced but her mind refused to accept them. The answers winked at her surreptitiously, even as they went about their convoluted ways to soften the edges for comfort.

The truth surfaced more naturally, through her body. It expressed itself in her health. It was the same truth that exploded in subtle ways in her novel *The Mandarins*. In the novel, a woman is nearing middle age. She has a young daughter. The woman who is the mother, returns home after bidding a last and final farewell to her lover, after they take a mutual resolution to stop meeting each other. The woman reaches home, locks herself inside her room for days on end and sits within, brooding over her life. Her young daughter tries her best to comfort her, she serves her meals, makes tea, pours wine and talks to her soothingly. But the woman seeks the privacy of her room and shuts herself in. After an interval, when she comes out, her appearance alarms her daughter. Is this my mother? How can she age so drastically, within a few days? She looks like a building that is in ruins. *My* mother? Who until now, in her late forties, had looked so very youthful, so very attractive. ..God, what's happened to mother?

Outside the novel, Sartre does not fail to notice the drastic change that has come over Simone. However, he turns to his girls and pursues his writing. Writes extensively. The Nobel Prize comes his way. He rejects it, and by doing so, his fame touches an all time peak. Half of the western world gets hooked on to his Existentialism. He writes a lot, struggling more and more with his failing health. And when he falls sick, Simone nurses him tenderly – like a mother, a sister, like a wife, or a faithful maid. Again the questions rose from within her and got quelled: what's this relationship? What's special about this?

Is there any real difference at all between living like this and living within the sanction of marriage, as husband and wife? Perhaps a man-woman relationship runs on a familiar, beaten path with these recognisable patterns and paradigms... ?

Simone gathered the silent questions together with the silent answers and offered them up to the next few generations to evaluate as they pleased. She offered her remarkable books – *The Second Sex, The Prime of Life, Force of Circumstances* and many, many more before she finally went to sleep.

"Uma, why are you nibbling at your food?" demanded Mangalam angrily. "At this age you should be eating well, you should have enough milk, butter, youghurt, sweets and so on. But look at you. You look pinched, you've become dark and thin. Is this what your great 'research' is all about?"

"Also, you've become rather listless, my child. What's the matter?" enquired her anxious father. "Take some leave. Let's all go out. Let's go home. I'll show you some beautiful temples."

"It's all because of you," said Mangalam, descending on her husband in rage. "I asked you to get her married by the month of *Thai* when we had such an excellent offer, but you wouldn't. You crawl through life and look what it has done to Uma."

Back stage sounds? They were loud and clear as the on-stage ones.

The telephone rang relentlessly. "What are you scratching your head about?" said an irate Shekar. "If you don't like the idea of Kashmir, let's go elsewhere. But leave the choice to me. I'll think of some nice, cool getaway."

"That's a wild, impossible idea," said Uma.

"What now! And here I am, thinking that you'll become like another Simone de Beauvoir, independent and bold. Hell! You're just a very ordinary girl, as ordinary as they come. Damn!"

His voice and the telephone calls retreated, faded off as background music, or more precisely, background sounds.

It was the late 1970s. Feminism as an 'ism' was still an emerging force which had started surfacing in different ways in different areas. Places swarmed with various seminars and conferences in departments of sociology, economics, literature, psychology and so on. In the literary forums, one repeatedly heard the names of Germaine Greer, Kate Millet, Gloria Steinem, Simone de Beauvoir amongst others. Literary scholars wrote about Simone as a fine example of one who lived her life like her books, of one who followed a unique lifestyle. Quite a few men also joined in the critical writings and discussions. That is how Uma happened to meet Mohan Mehta at a seminar in Chandigarh and later again, in Pune.

A lecturer in English, Mehta had a choice vocabulary. He could conceal himself behind the elegance of his expressions.

"Uma-ji, I've read some of your stories. As for your poems, I've even learnt a few of them by heart," he declared and went on to recite smoothly, the lines flowing out without a single mistake. Uma felt her goose-flesh prickling.

"Hush, don't. Please don't!" she protested.

"Sorry. I know how you feel. It would be embarrassing if someone were to hear me. Shall we go to the lounge? It's quiet in there."

They ordered some tea.

"How do you like this seminar?" he asked. "You know, I wanted to get up and ask the speakers why they go on and on citing western examples. Germaine Greer, Kate Millet, Simone de Beauvoir and what have you. Why don't they cite Indian women?" he asked, his face intense.

"Perhaps our women haven't attained an international reach yet. There have been some good writers, to be sure, but that's about all. No one has written anything that stimulates or provokes the consciousness of an entire nation, let alone the world. At least, not yet," said Uma.

"No, no, Uma-ji. Time will tell. We're a young country, but I've confidence in our women. Take someone like yourself, for instance. If writers like you try, you can really achieve this reach you talk about. Then you'll also be like a Simone de Beauvoir, some day."

Uma laughed.

"Why do you laugh? Because you haven't found a Sartre?"

Uma laughed even more, her shoulders shaking as she tried to control the laughter. She flicked away a tear that threatened to spill with her laughter.

"Mohan-ji, I'm surprised. Because just now you objected to our servile dependence on western models, western examples, and now you..."

"Heh, heh. ..actually, what I meant to say was that we should acknowledge our own writers, our literature first of all, although there is a lot to learn from the west. One can learn valuable things from the lives of Sartre and Simone. Come to think of it, Uma-ji, that we're born Indians is a mere accident, a freak of fate. True, we've our familial ties here, husband, wife, children, parents and so on. But to attain a quality in both writing and in life, we need to protect and preserve our individuality, you see. If you've no serious objection to the idea, we..."

Since then, Uma had counted many birthdays. It had been a time of search, just as it had also been a time of reckoning. Patterns appeared and reappeared, but with changing complexions, changing equations, changing values. The various seminars pushed into the front seasoned speakers who were articulate, smooth, even glib talkers. They invariably received a loud cheering and were applauded by the audience. Because the speakers said what the audience liked to hear.

For Uma, as for her peers, there were the usual pressures, of work, of career, of research, both institutional and private study. Things blew around her and her contemporaries, but she got a strange feeling that she was standing at the centre of it all, severely alone, absolutely alone. The 1970s rolled on towards the 80s and the 80s unfolded, bringing with them some confusions and half-truths that were perhaps characteristic of the times. Even for Mehta here, it must've surely been a time of uncertainties and uneasy truths, Uma conceded, silently.

"I can understand your hesitation, Uma-ji. I think I can guess the reason too, if I may say so. You may have heard this several times, right?"

"Oh, I could never even dream that I can be like another Simone de Beauvoir," said Uma, as calmly as she could.

"What about me? Do you think I can be like Sartre? Still, if we have the imagination, and the will..."

Swallowing the 1970s, the 80s reached the 90s. Now the 'ism' of Feminism took a foothold as a fierce movement. Newly recorded facts emerged from various disciplines, clinical psychology, agro-economics, eco-feminism, social anthropology, literature and the arts. They ignited sparks of cognition everywhere. The prescribed curricula in schools and colleges, the works of writers, films – just about everything came under a merciless re-evaluation. They were examined, analysed and judged unsparingly. Few areas escaped the new scrutiny.

Inside Levi jeans. Blue Lagoons, trousers or shorts, inside skirts, salwar-suits and stylishly trimmed hair a young femininity woke up on the strength of its own innate forces and impulses. Young women from different walks of life, with different cultural and professional conditioning, articulated their reactions with hard-headed clarity.

"Kate Millet really opened our eyes. Now we can never see D.H. Lawrence, or Henry Miller, or Jean Genet with the same eyes. We can't. Millet has stripped these writers stark naked and they now stand defenceless!" said a young girl. Her friends agreed with her. But they had no problems getting on with the young men they studied or worked with, or went out with. When the young women discussed things amongst themselves, one could see that Simone was not a forgotten figure.

"It was a fatal mistake on the part of Simone to have given herself, her entire life in fact, to Sartre on those terms," argued a young woman, hotly.

"Yes. A woman doesn't need a crutch to lean on in order to grow or develop in her art or in her writing. If only Simone had decided to stay alone, independent of Sartre, she would have evolved in more strikingly original ways."

"Maybe she would have then ushered in the new times earlier than she did."

"Yes. And yet, Simone was a fine intellectual. An excellent writer who not only had what's commonly termed 'intellectual honesty', but had the rarer thing, an emotional honesty. Sartre's oppressive presence eclipsed her somewhat, and dimmed her natural lustre. Simone should've got married to Nelson Algren, who was a damn decent guy. That would've been sensible. Then Sartre would've realised what 'Existentialism' was all about."

"Correct. We see this anomaly in our everyday life too. These men are torn apart by a paradox within themselves. Wonder how they handle it? Won't they split apart someday?"

"But they keep trying. When I was in the Mussoorie Academy for my IAS training, a guy told me that I was 'smart, talented' and that if I pair up with him, the two of us can show the world that we are 'yet another Simone-Sartre!' I smashed the mouldy myth that had wrapped around this couple and showed him what it was like for Simone, in reality.

Know how he reacted to that? He stopped talking to me, even stopped greeting me with a 'Hi' whenever he saw me," said the girl, laughing. Sounds of hearty laughter from the rest of the young women wafted on the air, borne aloft by the wind changing its course.

Even now, Simone continues to be a disconcerting presence, in her 'tangible absence'. She is analysed, probed, examined and argued about. Many of the new women are angry *for* her. They are angry about some of the decisions she took. Angry that a fine intellectual and sensitive writer like her should've lived with Sartre as less than a wife and with a blind devotion. It's all so unnecessary, they argue.

Slowly, time rolls out the balls of *pindam** on the smooth banana leaf. They show Simone in different colours as she retreats into some far-off point in the distant past. In between the rolling balls of *pindam*, whenever an occasion presents itself, Simone keeps tempting and seducing a Shekar or a Mehta or a young, potential bureaucrat in the Mussoorie Academy or wherever. She appears and re-appears.

***Pindam:** Balls of cooked rice offered to the manes in the Hindu ritual of obsequies in Tamil Nadu. The manes, i.e. the spirits of the ancestors, are worshipped as guardian influences.

Manju Kapur

Tara was fat. Her husband made it clear that it didn't do his image any good to have her waddling around, jiggling rolls of flesh.

"I dont waddle," she said, hurt.

"You do," said Abhay and that was the end of the matter. So far as words were concerned it was an established pattern that he had the last one.

Later she cried. She wiped away the tears that rolled down her soft, slightly flabby cheeks with a handkerchief clutched in a smooth, plump hand. She would like to be slim and svelte, a credit to her husband, but it was no use. Life without food, especially chocolate was not worth living.

Her husband couldn't be too serious about her losing weight, after all, he was her main supplier. She thought of his latest offering from Europe. Twenty bars of Swiss chocolate, seductively wrapped in green, orange, blue, and red, with gleaming pictures of fruit, nuts, and glasses of wine, rolls of marzipan, with a grainy paste of almonds covered with chocolate so smooth, it dissolved on the tip of her tongue, and the *piece de resistance*, two big boxes of cherries in liqueur set in cups of dark chocolate. Even when she wasn't eating them, she could feel in her mouth the sharpness of the liqueur, the bitter sweetness of the liquefying chocolate, the tanginess and gentle crunch of the cherry.

He was always assiduous in catering to her tastes. As he handed the chocolate to her he would tell her how busy he had been and how much he wished it were possible for her to accompany him. Then he would lightly rub the roll of fat around her belly to prove his love. At times the rub would get a little hard, but marks of physical affection between them were rare, and she took what she got.

When did it happen that Tara first got to know about her husband's affair? Something that the readers of this text will find obvious to the point of banality? A man who is stuffing his wife with chocolate in these quantities has to have an ulterior motive. A short history of her life will place her stupidity in perspective.

School: Ages 3-17. Convent, all girls. Strict emphasis on studies and nothing else. Tara's free time is taken with going to dance and music classes. Her mother says these things are important. Give grace to a girl.

College: Ages 17- 20. An all girls' college. Her parents don't think it wise to send Tara anywhere else. She chooses English Honours, considered a soft option. She isn't very clear what to do with her life, and English seems a good no-purpose subject. Besides she has always been fond of reading.

English Honours turns out to be not such a soft option after all. She had never thought reading could be so strenuous. Literature didn't seem to be about stories. All the emphasis was on ideas, history, context, marxist-feminist interpretations, and a pursuit of meaning that went beyond the obvious into the totally obscure.

Tara spends her time in college going to films with her friends, bunking classes. She complains to her mother about how hard her teachers expect her to work. Her mother consoles her. She has to somehow graduate, then she will get married.

The wedding preparations coincide with the prep leave for the exams.

"What to do, *beti*?" her mother says when Tara protests. "I know it is a bad time for you but then these are the auspicious dates."

"But Amma, how will I study?" complains Tara.

"Well the boy is good. And the family is very keen. Some things cannot be put off."

By the time Tara's results are out, she has come back from her honeymoon. She has got a third division, and is mildly surprised that she has passed at all.

Her husband thinks she is upset.

"Never mind, darling," he says clutching her in his strong, manly arms, "You have me."

Tara's heart beats fast, as she feels herself squeezed in that marital embrace.

"Yes, it's true," she whispers. "I have you."

The family then waits for the children to come. In time it becomes evident that if they came at all it would have to be through divine or medical intervention.

Tara started with the medical intervention front first.

"Maybe we should go and see a doctor?" she suggested to her husband.

"You go if you want to," replied Abhay. " There is nothing wrong with me."

After the doctor had examined Tara, she said there was nothing wrong with her either, and maybe a look at the husband was in order.

"But he doesn't think so," said Tara mournfully.

"What rubbish!" exclaimed the doctor, who was sick and tired of encountering such attitudes in her practice. "You tell him it is not only the woman who is responsible for bearing a child. The sperm has to be healthy. It may be that he is infertile, it may be that his sperm count is low, it may be that he has been drinking too much, or that he has some kind of latent infection. It may be any number of things."

Tara blushed. How was she supposed to convey all this to her husband?

Abhay agreed to see the doctor after a somewhat acrimonious discussion, in which he pointed out to Tara how completely wrong she was.

"Shouldn't I come too?" asked Tara, as Abhay was going.

"No," he said briefly. "I'll deal with it on my own."

So Tara never knew what happened at the doctor's. Abhay came home tight-lipped and cross, and refused to comment.

"But what *happened.* What did she *say*?" she asked several times.

"She's a fool. Huh! No point in your going to her either."

Medical consultations were not possible after this.

On the divine intervention front, Tara was told she should take a trip to Vaishno Devi crawling on her hands and knees.

After she had crawled up Vaishno Devi on her hands and knees, she decided to do the hands and knees stuff at other shrines. She had thought she would feel embarrassed, but she didn't. This was routine at these places.

Her husband thought all this was a great idea. So did her mother-in-law.

"Poor Tara!" she heard her say once. "She is trying so hard," and then in a lowered voice, "but she is unhealthy from the inside."

When there were no signs of conception after all this, Tara took to wearing certain stones around her neck and fingers, and her husband took to feeding her chocolates.

It was chocolate that drew her attention to a certain lack of something on the part of Abhay. He became casual in getting her what she wanted.

After an excess of peppermint she hinted that she would look forward to more variety. He had complained.

"I don't get the time," he said. "All I can do is pick up these things from the airport, and peppermint is what airports happen to have."

"But so much?"

She turned the green and white boxes over in her hands. Edwardian Mints, Creme de Menthe Mints, Bitter Chocolate Mints, Wafer Mints, After Eight Mints, After Dinner Mints, Mints in White Chocolate.

She felt sick at the idea of this much mint. But her craving for chocolate was so strong that she ate them all anyway.

And then he did it again.

"Didn't you remember?" she asked.

"What?" He looked preoccupied.

"What I said last time. About the mints."

"Last time? Oh, oh, yes, of course. But you see the airports..."

She looked at all that revolting peppermint.

"But before you managed ..."

"Well you know these airports. Not very imaginative."

That's not what Tara would have thought as she remembered the brochures that Abhay frequently got advertising this airline, that airport. They seemed to contain virtually everything under the sun.

After Abhay left, Tara remained lost in thought. It was odd that he had forgotten her request – her reasonable request – about the mint chocolate. Abhay had a good memory. But then he was always so preoccupied. And hardly ever at home.

And in between these two thoughts, sequences in a chain, suspicion pounced and bent the links in another direction.

Within a matter of seconds, Tara was convinced she had found the clue to much of Abhay's behaviour. Could it be, could it be that what she had read about in her college days, could it be that the Other Woman had appeared in her life as well? She made up her mind to spy on him. The results were predictable.

After she had gone through the gamut of emotions ranging from shock, confusion, despair, anger and resentment, she toyed with the idea of knocking her brains out. To help reach a conclusion she automatically went to the fridge to take out her chocolates. She needed consolation. Absent-mindedly she bit into one. It tasted like sawdust. She bit into it again and gagged. This was the only pleasure she had in her life. What was happening to it?

She felt a burning sensation at the back of her throat, and the sour ugly taste of bile. She quickly put the chocolate back into the fridge and closed the door. Nausea overcame her, and she barely made it to the bathroom.

She never ate another piece of chocolate again. Everytime she looked at the dark shining pieces glistening invitingly at her, she saw Abhay's eyes sunk in them, tempting her to bite into a piece and get fat.

She lost weight. The feeling of nausea she had about chocolate helped put her off eating. She grew thinner, thinner than she had been in years. She took the rings off her fingers. There seemed little point in wearing them now. From saris she moved to *salwar-kameez*. She looked younger. She felt more alert and alive than she had for a long time. She began to think about strategies.

She must win him back she thought. She decided to join cooking classes. The way to a man's heart was through his stomach. Abhay hardly ate at home. But now.... She must cook. She would be the source of all things delectable.

Tara joined Mrs. Singhal's Cooking Classes, which guaranteed mastery of Cordon Bleu, Continental, Chinese and Indian cuisines in just a year. Tara discovered in herself a light hand, and a flair for improvisation. Her teacher praised her too, and that helped. No one had ever praised her learning anything in her life, academics was out of the question, and even her dancing and singing teachers had felt that she needed to apply herself more.

For Mrs. Singhal a meal was not just eating. It was an Aesthetic Experience. The table, the colours, the setting, the flowers, everything had to be perfect.

Tara dived into Experience like a duck into water. Cooking was endlessly creative she discovered. The taste which she had exhibited in doing up her home, had scope that was infinitely various on the site of the dining table. She experienced the joys of putting before a husband – however errant – things he could not resist. He became quite greedy and demanding, entertaining small numbers of friends more often at home.

Imperceptibly Abhay began to put on weight. Tara could see for herself the fruit of her labours, and her sense of power grew. New thoughts began to enter her head. She increased the cream in her desserts and began putting more cheese in the Italian dishes. Abhay's clothes did not fit him any more. He began to talk seriously of dieting.

At this point Tara looked him over speculatively. In her mind's eye she saw him as she herself had once been. "You waddle," he had said at the beginning of the story, and she predictably female, had replied in pain, "I do not." Now she wanted him to waddle, though her position might not allow her to rub his nose in the fact as he had done hers.

When Abhay's affair broke up, a certain moroseness tinged and deepened the yellow of his already saturnine complexion. For consolation he turned to serious eating. He listened to music, he drank, and he demanded hot and spicy tit-bits from Tara's ever fertile kitchen.

When he began to waddle, she, trained to find her husband beautiful in all his manifold aspects, started to find him ugly.

Given the circumstances of her revenge, she needed an affair to give it a finished ending. She chose a friend of his, the most convenient male to hand. The friend had dropped certain hints, Tara decided to pick them up. She indulged herself with him without taking precautions. She had long given up the possibility of conceiving, and when she found herself pregnant, she was exhilarated. The first thing to do was to get rid of the friend.

"Abhay suspects," she told him.

Then she told her husband, "I think perhaps it has been your improved health," she said. "You look so much better now: Before you were too thin. That is why I have been blessed with this baby."

A puzzled look crossed Abhay's face as he took in the air of quiet triumph in his wife's manner. He started spying on her, but her affair had been so brief and circumspect that he found no traces of it.

When Tara's daughter was born, she crooned her lullabies of brave women warriors, and made sure that all her education was oriented towards a career that would make her independent.

Twenty or Twenty-Five?

Madhu Kishwar

For Heaven's sake, Bhagwati, must you go around looking so miserable? So what if you've lost one house? You'll soon find another!"

"It's not so easy. It'll take at least 15 to 20 days, even a month. How will I manage till then? Bhagwati answered, dejection writ large on her face, tears filling her eyes.

How strangely attached Minna is to this Bhagwati! If Bhagwati seems even slightly depressed, Minna grows restless, almost begins to blame herself. She may even end up scolding Bhagwati: "Why should you make yourself miserable over that good for nothing fellow? It's not as if he's of any use to you. You're earning your own living. So why don't you just forget about him, and stay happy?"

Sermons of this kind make Bhagwati smile. Sadly. What can

she say ? She, whose husband has never contributed a paisa to running the house, nor spoken a decent word to her in ten years of married life. Sure, he forces a child on her every year or two. And also gives her a thrashing every second day. As for her mother-in-law and sister-in-law, they turn away their faces, like Bapu's monkeys who have sworn to see no evil and hear no evil. But if Bhagwati ever dares say a word in reply to her husband's ravings, they hear her fast enough. Both of them pounce on her : "You shameless hussy talking back to your husband!"

Perhaps Bhagwati would put up with all this, but there, is one insult which makes her blood boil. On the one hand, this man keeps giving her one child after another, climbs on to her whenever he feels like it, beats and kicks her when she resists, yet on the other hand, he has a mistress too. Sometimes he disappears for a night, sometimes for a whole week. That's where all his earnings go. Of course, when he has thrown away his own earnings on drink, he can always beat up Bhagwati and snatch the little money she has, to give to that other woman.

If one advises such an ill starred woman to stay happy, will it not seem as if one must be joking? So Bhagwati smiles. The smile seems to say: "Happiness is for *bibis* like you, who have every comfort, whose husbands come and hand over their salaries to you, and never say a harsh word. Where can women like me find happiness ?"

Her sad smile hurts Minna like a taunt. Whenever Bhagwati comes to work with a bruised body and swollen eyes, Minna starts tingling with anger, and bursts out: "Why can't you leave that good for nothing wretch? After all, you earn enough to feed, yourself, don't you?" "Maybe I can wash dishes and earn enough to feed the children, but where will I stay? Rent for the smallest of huts is Rs 100. How can I pay Rs 100 for a hut out of a total of 150 ? In any case our *biradari* people will make my life even more of a hell if I start living alone. Women can't do such things in our community."

Minna and Bhagwati have repeated this conversation dozens of times. It is Bhagwati who gets beaten up, but it is Minna who flies into a rage. Sometimes she feels exasperated with Bhagwati. Why must she look so forlorn and dejected ? Why doesn't she feel any anger? There she is, working away, dejected, mechanical. And she will do as much work as you ask her to. She just doesn't know how to say 'No.' That's why the *bibis* in all the five houses where she works are in a constant state of mingled annoyance and affection. Once she goes into a house to work, there is no knowing when she will emerge and proceed to the next house.

But perhaps Bhagwati has, a special fondness for Minna. And why does Minna get so perturbed when she sees Bhagwati depressed? How easy it is to get exasperated and say: "Why don't you leave that wretch?" but the words which should follow stick in her throat : "You can come and stay with me..." How many times she has thought of saying that, but has not been able to work up the courage. Where can she possibly accommodate Bhagwati and her three children? True, there are three rooms in the house, but Minna has three children of her own, besides her husband's young brother staying with them. The children have already started saying they need a separate room for study. The saving grace, she thinks, is that they managed to rent this house five years ago at Rs 650 a month. If they look for another house like this one now, they'll have to pay at least Rs 1,500. Sure, her husband is a government officer, and earns Rs 1,900 a month. He keeps Rs 400 for his personal expenses and hands over Rs 1,500 to Minna. It's up to her to manage the house on that. The family is small – two boys, one girl. But it seems to her that the Rs 1,500 is hardly in her hands before it is all gone – 650 for houserent, 250 for the children's school fees. And 600 left over for the whole month's rations, milk, vegetables, electricity, water, and dozens of small things like soap, oil, toothpaste.

And how is she to make the same Rs 600 pay for the children's books, summer and winter uniforms, shoes, socks ? Minna doesn't remember a single month when all three children at the same time had a decent pair of new shoes each. How could they, when the most ordinary pair of shoes for a two-year-old costs Rs 35? Minna almost shrinks from going to the market. A shopping trip sends her into a depression. At home, Rs 300 looks like such a big sum. One thinks one can buy a great many things with it. But when you reach the market and start asking prices, your heart begins to sink: "Peas Rs 8 a kilo, Rs 12 for a packet of Surf, even a pair of socks for a small child costs not less then Rs 6!"

Only Minna knows how difficult it is for her to eke out 30 days on those Rs 1,500 and what mental acrobatics it involves. The newspaper is full of comments on deficit financing whenever a new budget or five year plan is being floated. Minna often wonders how the government will ever manage to repay the crores of deficit that accumulate each year. If she's even 15 days late in paying the grocer's bill, how embarrassed she feels to go to the market ! Her husband feels he has done his duty once he has handed over Rs 1,500 to her. He also feels entitled to expect at least *dal,* one vegetable and *raita* at every meal. As well as special dishes on Sundays and holidays. There was a time when *pulao and raita* were considered a special Sunday meal. Now he turns up his nose at it. "Oh lord, that same old *pulao !* Why can't you learn to make something interesting, like noodles, for example?"

Last Sunday, she made *kheer,* and he was ready with his nasty comment : "What was the use of my looking for an educated, modern wife, if I am doomed to spend my life eating *kheer ?* Why don't you read *Femina* or *Eve's Weekly*? Last week, I was leafing through one of them and I saw a recipe for a fantastic pineapple pudding. Or why don't you take a cue from Mrs Mehra – she's always turning out a Chinese meal, or a French pudding. After all, there ought to be a difference between your cooking and my mother's cooking. You're an educated, modern woman!"

Minna has grown so used to hearing such speeches that she doesn't think it necessary to answer. In the early years of their marriage, there used to be heated arguments whenever Ravi made such remarks. Here she was, emerging hot and bothered from the kitchen, and there he was, ready with a new sarcasm each day. She would fling a retort at him : "Why don't you go get yourself a five star cook from Hotel Maurya, or better still, go and marry a cook? Here the kids need socks, and Sonu has to have a winter uniform. Should I worry about that, or about your noodles?"

Ravi would flare up immediately: "Time enough to worry about their socks when you are through with your saris and fashions."

Hearing this, Minna would feel as if she was on fire, body and spirit. How she longed to pick up the bowl of *kheer* and throw it in Ravi's face. But how could she, when she knew it would be a good six months before they could afford to buy a new bowl? Hot tears of helplessness would sting her eyes as she spat back: "Who's talking of saris? I haven't been able to buy myself a single blouse from your salary in these five years! I'm still wearing the clothes my mother gave me."

That was enough to make Ravi pick up the bowl of *kheer,* hurl it to the floor, and stamp out of the house. What a fine end to the special Sunday lunch! Ravi could smash the bowl and then storm out. What was there for Minna to smash – her own head?

But how long can one carry on like this, smashing crockery, and fighting like cats and dogs? What with the children watching, and picking up their father's ways, gradually Minna had to teach herself to swallow her anger and remain silent. Now she either turns a deaf ear to Ravi, or offers herself a reasonable explanation for his behaviour: "Poor fellow, he works so hard all day. Naturally, he expects a good meal when he returns home." She tries to save money in every possible way. When Rahul's sweater tears, she unravels and reknits it into a warm vest for Sonu. instead of giving the children's clothes to the tailor, she stitches them at home. She used to love reading, but since the children came, she hasn't been able to buy herself a single book. She consoles herself by thinking:

"This is not the age for me to read. It's enough if we can somehow manage to educate the children."

Educating them is hard enough now that a four- year-old's tuition fees are Rs 75 plus busfare, uniforms, books, notebooks, and dozens of incidentals. Far from buying herself a sari, months often pass before she can bring herself to buy a new pair of slippers, when the old pair gets torn. "How often do I go out ? At home, anything will do," she tells herself, "And even when I do go out, my sari hides my slippers." As for saris, her mother gives her one or two a year, or her brother sends her one at Diwali. She is so careful with them that her marriage saris still look good as new. When a sari does get worn out, Minna can't bear to throw it away, so she stitches it into curtains.

In spite of all this, she has to hear the same irritable remarks : "Heaven knows how you manage to make a whole month's salary disappear in 15 days !" At such times, Minna reminds herself that she is more fortunate than are many others. At least, Ravi always hands over the major part of his salary to her. Just look at poor Uma next door. Every morning, she has to tell her husband what she needs to buy, whether milk or vegetables, and he then puts the exact price of it into her hands. On days when he is in a temper, he doesn't even deign to do that. The poor thing has no idea how much her husband earns. Ravi has never humiliated her by making her beg for each five rupee note, nor has he ever asked her to account for what she spends. He keeps only Rs 400 for himself, and he too has difficulty managing. By the end of the month, Minna usually has to pay for his cigarettes from the vegetable budget.

After the tenth of the month, when she has paid all the bills, Minna has to stop and think every time she spends a rupee.

But today was only the third of the month, so Minna was feeling quite carefree.When she saw Bhagwati nearly in tears, Minna couldn't restrain herself. "How much did that *bibi* pay you?"

"She paid Rs 25. That was the money with which I bought vegetables once a day. In the morning I give the children dry *roti* with salt, but in the evening they like to have a little *dal* or vegetable. Now what will I eat and what will I feed them, out of Rs 125?"

The words slipped out of Minna's mouth : "Listen, you wash the clothes in my house from this month." Then your children needn't go without their vegetable." She had said it – and she had wanted to say it – but immediately she felt upset. "Another added expenditure. And she's sure to use more washing soap than I do. If I'd just asked her to wash the clothes, she'd have happily agreed to do it for 15 or 20 rupees. But now perhaps she'll expect me to pay 25 since the job she has lost used to pay her Rs 25." But looking at Bhagwati's tearful face, Minna couldn't bring herself to do such petty bargaining. How could she haggle over five or ten rupees when confronted with that sad face?

So from the third of the month, Bhagwati began to wash the clothes as well, besides continuing to wash the dishes and clean the house. Minna had been paying her Rs 50 a month for those two jobs. Minna feels quite pleased that this payment is higher than the "rate" prevailing in the colony. There is not really so much work to be done in her house. Minna never cooks lunch on weekdays. The children come home from school at 4, Ravi and his brother return around 6.30. In the morning, she prepares a packed lunch for each of them. Why cook lunch just for herself at noon? She manages with a cup of tea. After all, she rarely gets to have breakfast before 11.30. When everyone leaves at 9, the house looks as if it has been hit by a tornado – dirty clothes lying all around, wet towels on the beds, one of Sonu's socks under the bed and the other out on the verandah, Ravi's soiled vest draped on the sofa or thrown on the ironing table. It takes her at least two hours every day to set the house in order. Bhagwati is supposed to do the cleaning, but is sweeping and mopping all the cleaning that is required?

Minna gets up at 6 in the morning and starts preparing for the five of them to leave. When they finally depart at 9, she feels as if she has entertained a marriage party and sent it on its way. Ravi is no better than a child. He can't even take his own clothes out of the cupboard. Voices echo all around "Mummy, where is this? Minna, where is that?"

After tidying the house, Minna spends one and a half hours washing the clothes. She tries to get an hour's rest in the afternoon. But her mind refuses to rest. It recalls that Sonu's vest has to be mended or Ravi's shirt has to have new buttons stitched on. From 6 in the morning to 11 at night, there is always something or other to be done.

The work never shows any signs of getting finished. Now that the children are somewhat older, she gets six or seven hours' sleep at night. When they were small, night and day seemed to merge into each other. Minna felt like a nurse who for years has been on

24-hour emergency duty, without casual leave, without sick leave, without a Sunday off.

Now that Bhagwati has started washing the clothes, Minna gets a couple of hours' rest in the afternoon. She borrows some books from the lending library, but ten years of not reading seem to have taken their toll. She finds it hard to concentrate, even on a novel. After reading four or five pages, her eyes begin to shut. She has been working non stop from 6 to 12. Where is she to find the energy to read ? Well, at least she manages a nap.

The dilemma continued in her mind: "How much should I pay her for washing the clothes? Rs 15 is too little. I think 20 should be all right. But she must be expecting 25. It's all my fault – I should have put things more clearly."

As it was Minna found it difficult to pay Rs 50. She often thought that if she were to do the dishwashing and the cleaning herself; she could save some money and buy some fruit for the children. But 75! The thought of it made Minna regret her soft heartedness.

On a day when there was a big heap of soiled clothes, bedsheets and bedcovers to be washed, Minna's heart would melt: "Poor thing, where does she get the energy to do the work of five houses? I find it hard enough to manage my own." This feeling would lead her to decide: "I'll give her Rs 25. Let her make something out of the deal."

But on a day when there chanced to be fewer clothes, Minna would begin hesitating all over again. "Rs 25 for a few clothes like these. And they're hardly even dirty. All one has to do is soak them and rinse them out. No one else would pay her more than 15. I'll give her 20 – that's more than enough. In any case, what about all the other things I do for her. I gave her an old sari last month, and I'm always giving her the children's outgrown clothes. These days, how many people would give away old clothes when one can get a good steel bowl in exchange for three old saris."

Once she got into this frame of mind, she would reckon up every cup of tea, every left over scrap of food or old sari given to Bhagwati, and would end up feeling quite pleased with herself for her noble, charitable impulses. "After all, 1 give her a cup of tea every day. Such a big cup of tea would cost at least 50 paise in the market. And then I give her all the leftover food, even though left overs don't go bad these days. I could easily keep them in the fridge and use them two days later."

Every day, sometimes several times a day, Minna's mind would swing like a pendulum between 20 and 25. The day Bhagwati took a holiday, Minna would decide on 20. But the day Minna had guests and Bhagwati uncomplainingly washed piles of dishes, or the day Minna cleared out the storeroom and Bhagwati spent an extra hour helping her, Minna would feel ashamed of herself. "Poor thing, she never calculates the way I do. She ungrudgingly does all the extra work I pile on her, yet I am so stingy with every five rupees 1 give her. I don't worry about the money spent on the kids. I'd cheerfully spend my last paisa on them, Yet who knows, when they grow up, they'll probably turn their backs on us."

But the dilemma persisted. Was it at all possible to resolve it?

If one considered what Bhagwati needed and deserved, even Rs 50 would be too little. Minna well knew how much energy goes into washing clothes. "But how can I be responsible for her needs?" she would think irritably. "Why has she gone and produced three children, when she doesn't know where her next meal is coming from?"

Her irritation couldn't last long, however. She well remembered the day when Bhagwati's husband had beaten her black and blue because she had gone with Minna to the hospital, and had had herself fitted with a loop. He hadn't given Bhagwati any peace till she got the loop removed.

When she saw Bhagwati look tired and ill fed, Mina often felt like giving her a glass of milk, but then she would think of her own children : "They are hardly swimming in milk and butter," and she would stop herself.

By the 29th of the month, Minna had still been unable to resolve the dilemma of whether to pay 20 or 25. She tried to shake herself out of it : "Why am I acting so petty and mean ? As if a saving of five or ten rupees will make such a great difference to the house ! Anyway, who is going to give me any credit for such an accomplishment?"

It was easy to give herself a sermon, but she knew that it was only by saving such small sums that she was able to maintain the veneer of "respectability" in their household. She had never let herself spend Rs 2.50 on a scooter even when she came home from the market, laden with three heavy shopping bags full of the month's rations. No, she would wait half an hour in the hot sun and travel in a jampacked bus. Then how could she so easily bring herself to spend Rs 25 on getting clothes washed?

That day, Ravi came home in a very good mood. "Minna, remember Rakesh, that old friend of mine? He's been transferred to Delhi. I've invited the whole family to lunch on Sunday – that's day after tomorrow. Just see that there's a real *daawat,* OK? He's a very good friend of mine. Whenever I've been to Kanpur, he's entertained me like a prince. Don't forget to make chicken curry."

Minna gazed openmouthed at him. "My dear sir, do you realise that you are ordering this feast on the 29th of the month ? Where do you think the money for the chicken is going to come from?"

"Oh come on, don't give me that line. As if I don't know that women always put by a nest egg from their husbands' salaries. And Rakesh isn't just any friend. He's a very special friend."

It was useless to argue, so she fell silent. And sure enough – the chicken, the *pulao,* the jelly and custard were all prepared, besides the usual *dal* and vegetables.

"If this is what makes him happy, well and good. After all, he's earning the money. What right do I have to refuse?"

Minna immersed herself in preparations for the guests. Everything went off well on Sunday, but in the midst of the gaiety, suddenly Minna's face grew pale. Where had Ravi got those four bottles of beer from ? Two days ago, he had asked Minna to lend him money for cigarettes. Struck by a thought, Minna put down the dish she was holding, and went into the bedroom. She opened the cupboard and exclaimed aloud in anger. Her small piggy bank was lying there – open, empty. All the money she had saved up so painfully, by selling old newspapers and old tins – gone. She had intended to buy Sonu's winter uniform with that money I She felt like going and hitting Ravi on the head with the piggy bank. Paralysed by rage, she sat there without moving for a good 20 minutes. She altogether forgot that she had put the chicken curry on the gas stove, to get warmed up. After a while, Ravi called out: "Hey madam, have you gone off to sleep or what? Can't you smell the chicken burning?"

Minna got up, startled. Why throw a tantrum in front of guests? When she went into the drawing room, she had the same smile plastered on her face, she was once more the ideal wife and gracious hostess.

After lunch, Rakesh and Ravi sat down to cards, while Rakesh's wife helped Minna to clear away. There was a whole heap of dishes. Bhagwati had spent the afternoon at Minna's house, to help out with the extra work. As per Minna's instructions, she had worn specially washed clothes, in honour of the guests. Two days ago, her husband had beaten her badly, because she had admitted her eldest daughter into school, without taking his permission. Her body was still covered with bruises, and her left elbow was aching. Still she had mopped the floor twice over today, and washed all the crockery with great care. She had peeled the vegetables, and ground the spices for Minna. She finished her work in the other houses as quickly as possible so as to be back in time to help Minna serve the food. It was three in the afternoon, and Bhagwati was still busy in the kitchen.

"You have your lunch first, and wash the dishes afterwards,"

Mina told her. She heaped a plate for Bhagwati, and then set to cleaning the kitchen shelves. After a short while, she sensed that Bhagwati had finished eating. Without turning to look at her, Minna said in a low voice: “Listen. From tomorrow, you need not wash the clothes. I’ll wash them myself. I get fed up with having nothing to do all day long.” And with that, she hastily went out of the kitchen.

Fig Blossom

Sukrita Paul Kumar

The fig tree and I grew up together in the garden. We are both situated at one end of the garden. The back garden. In the front, in that huge bungalow lives Minu who does not play with me. For fear of messing her starched dresses. But Chintu steals out sometimes, not caring for what he gets when he goes back into the house. Their mother is a doll with honey smiles at the front door and a screeching witch at the back door, hounding and threatening whoever came her way. I have always thought of her as two different women!

My fig tree and I. Fresh air, some rain and a bit of sunshine... that's all that was needed to make us rise from the ground. We have no brothers or sisters. If they do exist, we know not what may have become of them. We have after all each other to love, and to quarrel with. I remember how I would pull at those tender arms branching out of him in all directions. And he'd pinch my baby-skin bloody red with the milk spurting out of its cracking limbs. I called them white tears. I wish I could produce them too. Mine were so inane and colourless and ineffective. Nobody would ever notice them.

Amma has been washing the pots and pans of the big house day after day. From the time she was thrown out on the streets by that quiet burly man with his eyes popping out. All those long, dragging days, those eyes had hung over me, heavy with love. I lay groaning in the clutches of some devil; he focussed, glared and shooed the fever away. He cared. Amma was always busy with Kanti. Every day some time in the morning, he walked into the house with heavy army boots demanding immediate attention, "Hey, fetch me a glass of water", "Go get me some tea", or "can't you give me some rag to wipe my sweating forehead?" and then he would grumble, "this brat of yours will never learn to attend to one coming from outside" after which he'd burst out, "Wait till I lay my hands on you." "A spoilt *chhokra*!" I clenched my teeth, itched to punch his belly but helplessly tried to avoid him. He was a bully. But I had a silent bonding with the other man, the one with grey eyes. I knew he was my father though Amma tried to convince me that it was Kanti and that I should love him.

I never liked Kanti, the man who would twirl the thick bushes of his moustaches that crept into his nostrils whenever he broke into his loud guffaws. The bushes would droop back heavily on his lips the moment he stopped laughing. God knows how many progeny Kanti had scurried into Amma's dreams filling her with promises of his future prosperity. Amma, so wise and clear-headed, could not see what I, a child of four years, could so easily perceive. Kanti was a hoax, a fraudulent lover who may have declared himself a slave of many women, only to be a diabolic master of all. He kept coming to Amma even after we landed in the shanty given to her as the utensil cleaner of the big house. One day Kanti disappeared. Just like that. But long before he went away his fearsome moustaches had succeeded in shunting me out of that dark hole, "my home". I would keep away outside, away into the other corner where my friend, the fig tree had been planted the very day we had come to this house. Amma was made to carry several bags of soil from the other end of the garden for the infant fig sapling to find its roots. I planted myself next to it happily. Amma and Kanti could not help demonstrating their pleasure at having me out of the way. I had actually found my own freedom and my own companion.

I had craved for this... the freedom to allow the image of the 'burly man' come to my mind as my father, the freedom to talk about him with my only friend swinging on its already firm roots and by now reaching the height of my waist. With me on my knees, we'd be face to face: "Hey, Bachoo!" I've always called him Bachoo, the little one, as I was so much bigger when we first met. "Bachoo, I see those grey eyes out of their sockets planted in the black sky of the night staring down at me. That man had cared for me quietly. That look goes deep into me. How can he not be my father? I could not be anybody else's. Kanti and Amma had turned him wild. He suddenly awakened and threw her out. Me too, I also drove her out of myself then. You know, Bachoo, those eyes and I share so much!"

Bachoo let a whiff of air rustle through its tender leaves in perfect communion. And then, there would be moments of tangible silence, my eyes welling up, and I'd gradually change my position, lie flat on the ground with my palm feeling Bachoo's tough roots covered by the soft ground... Bachoo, my friend... Bachoo, my son.... Bachoo, my father...

I felt my branches swinging with Bachoo's till we'd both be lulled into another world, the world where Kanti did not matter, and Amma too was not visible. But soon their images would crawl back into me like termites, when Amma would suddenly come and shake me: "There you are again! Always lying around in this comer. Why can't you hear me the first time? Come, have your *roti*... I have to rush back... Memsahib's got some guests. And remember. You are not to be seen by them... remain at the back. I'll pull your ears red if my Memsahib finds you anywhere around and I get to pay for it. Don't even venture to the front of the house, or I'll break your legs!" Amma's face, the face of a ferocious cat, loomed over me with her bright red tongue flapping quickly, and the frowning forehead dancing over her fiery eyes. The very same Amma, who used to turn into a gentle cow in the presence of that man Kanti. It was some mesmerism. Whether I actually went and ate that *roti* was not her anxiety. But I did learn to eat for my survival. Whenever my body demanded, I would go up to the shanty and locate a half-dried *chapati*, sometimes even half-eaten by mice. But that was not to go on for long. Because soon, I explored the huge back garden which had much more to offer: green mangoes and raw guavas, carrots and radishes! Even Bachoo, had gained such height in just two or three years that it overtook me and showered all his love for me into his fruit ... the deep red figs which I devoured.

"Bachoo! I too want to create such capsules of love. I too want to glut you with love..." and Bachoo would shed some more of its figs as though unable to contain the abundance. In the sweltering heat of the summer months, I would often bring buckets of water to bathe Bachoo's dusty leaves and pour it on the dry cracking earth, over its roots, around the base of its trunk. I would pour the water slowly, watching it rush into the cracks impatiently. I specially enjoyed doing this because there was always such shortage of water and most of the garden was left half-thirsty by Puttu-da, the *maali* who'd come early in the morning to tend to the plants. For emergency, there was a tank full of water stored in the backyard, from where I stole some each day for my dear old Bachoo, who looked so parched with just a few hours of the scorching sun. When I ran the bucket of water over Bachoo, my soul danced in glee, bathed in streams of joy.

With the very first monsoon showers, there are rows of big, glistening black ants crawling on Bachoo's sturdy trunk. They march out of their holes as soldiers in helmets celebrating freedom from the steaming earth. They look so disciplined. Once, when I clasped a thick branch and my fingers came in their way, they didn't like it at all. Their movement was disturbed by the enemy. They panicked and ran all over my fingers, creeping up my arm, and finding their way to the rest of my body, biting and stinging wherever they got a chance. They clung on with their stings hooked into me, each sending a lightning pain down my spine. One by one, I pulled them out and crushed them with a stone in utter vengeance... the crackling sound startled me. And then, rows of them reached out to their dead comrades, lifting and dragging the corpses ceremoniously, in respect for the dead. I have never had the patience to see exactly where they took their dead. I know they don't abandon them. Such battalions of them. Bachoo seemed most unaffected. Not even a leaf would stir while scores of those little monsters would be biting through the bark making deep holes into it.

I reached the insides of one such hole after watching them crawl into it in one continuous line for a long time. In the darkness of that dome, I saw those eyes shining, the eyes of my Abbu popping out at me. "Come, my son, I have been waiting..." And then that deep sigh, ... my fever, the devil and he, my saviour. I stayed with him for a long time, with no words between us. I tried to remember the sound of his voice. Always, what I hear are eerie sounds of exasperation or the silent sighs of love. Nothing in between.

The black hole was so warm, and... and... cosy, so much like home. But the wide, open sunlight behind me called out and loomed over me with naked threats. And my Abbu. "Why son, why do you have to go? Stay!" The voice trailed through the dark, from the very heart of Bachoo. Those eyes ... he is so safe in there. I cannot be there for long ... that is, if I want to preserve it all. One day Memsahib's eyes fell on me when I was with my Abbu. "You there, you good-for-nothing brat! Why can't you help your good-for-nothing mother inside? Another one of those sacks of rotten potatoes like you! Such lords... as if they own this place!"

I dragged myself away from Abbu, came out into the sunlight baffled, and ran to reach Amma panting. She stood scrubbing the utensils vigorously, with all her anger and fire in her hands while the water gushed out of the tap with full force. She lifted her left arm to wipe her sweating forehead with one end of her sari *pallu*, while I pulled at the other. "Amma, Amma, listen to me, Amma!" I whispered to her urgently, snuggling closer and closer to her. Only I could get her out of her misery. I thought the time had come. "Amma, I'll take you to Abbu... let's finish this work and get out." She had been totally oblivious of me till now, getting consumed in her own fire. Suddenly she was alerted. I thought I saw anger slipping out of her. Her forehead knitted into deep thought, she frowned, was almost startled. This was the first time I had mentioned Abbu to her. I had crossed into the forbidden zone.

She paused, looked deep into my eyes and then all at once, she raised her arm as if to strike me. She changed her mind and pinched me hard into my side. "*Soo..er ke bacche*! Why can't you leave me alone ... as if I don't have enough problems feeding you. I have always known ... you have never belonged to me. To come plaguing me about what you call Abbu! Let me tell you today, he is dead and thankfully gone. They found him dead drunk and breathing his last on the streets, a long time ago. And you will take me to him! *Maaf karo*, I want to live and find my Kanti. I will not stop you, you can go to the dead!"

Amma had become a total wreck by now. Kanti had smothered all life out of her but she continued to pin all her hopes on his coming back. And now, I had found my Abbu, my home, my Bachoo and had nothing to do with the inhabitants, or their doings, inside Amma's room. Those four walls did not mean anything to me. Amma and her thoughts of Kanti filled up every nook and comer. Her presence somehow included the presence of Kanti. This kept me away from the room, from Amma and indeed from Kanti. That is what I wanted the most. With Kanti gone, Amma's behaviour towards me did not change. In fact she was all the more irritable and resentful with me after he stopped coming. As for Abbu, he had never existed for her anyway. His death then made no difference. She never even mentioned his death to me. All the better. Yes, Abbu's death would make no difference to me either. Since for me he'd always be there. To either of us then, the news of his death would not change the situation. He remained intact in the dark depth of the nightly skies, as also in the black ant-hole, in the warmth of Bachoo's heart.

Why had I reached out to Amma? She had looked so sad and forlorn. I thought Abbu and I could support her. She had no idea about the home I shared with Bachoo, and now with Abbu too. Little did she know about me... or my sounds, the voices, the eyes, the figs, the ants ... She barked at my offer. Is she right? Does she know more? Is she wiser? I don't care. She certainly does not know what I know and what I feel. The boundaries between us are steadfast. Occasionally, Amma and I come out of our worlds, into the no-man's land in between. Only to realise again, the separateness of our existence and then to withdraw quickly, unable to cope with the shadow of the other.

Now onwards I found myself a prey to Memsahib's wish to see me working, to extract as much work out of me as possible. "Why can't you take a brush and scrub the floor today?" "Go, remove the cobwebs from the verandah, your mother never gets time for that!", "Puttu has not come today, surely you can water the plants today!" She always thought of some chore for me. The price I had to pay for living in her garden! "Bachoo, watch out, if she could have her way, she'd make you sweep her floors ... may her eyes not fall on you my friend..." Flocks of twittering birds would fly out of Bachoo's mass of green when he giggled and shook his branches in protest.

Bachoo had spread out like an emperor. Tall, well-built and muscular, with broad, big and deep green leaves waving proudly and majestically. Like elephant ears. The legendary fig-leaves! OK, I see the point. I have had a long, ancestral relationship with Bachoo. Lying under the dense foliage, I looked up and saw bits of the blue sky spilling and peeping down at me ... the strong summer sun weakened and cooled through Bachoo. And then, through the figs, the leaves and the branches, through the tree itself, I see those eyes again ... the eyes that dig into my bare soul, pouring love into my blood stream, arousing my nerves and capturing me totally. "My son, you are with me. We are together. We are family. My boy..." They say Abbu is dead! But he is more alive than ever. I look intently into those eyes. Is there death anywhere in them? Not a trace of it. I do not blink lest I lose him. I look, keeping looking as I rise to reach out... to Abbu through Bachoo. "Bachoo ... don't stir..." I whisper under my breath, my skin taut with anxiety, "Don't move ... I don't want him to disappear..."

I rise up on the tips of my toes, stretching myself to the fullest, my arms raised. I see more than the eyes now ... the contours of the rest of Abbu ... the space around, filling up with him. On the tree ... on top of the figs, over the canopy, rest Abbu's feet. I feel them as I climb my way up, hugging Bachoo. The black ants crawl all over me. I too crawl with the ants around the black holes, my eyes tied to Abbu's, my limbs around Bachoo. As I reach the top, flocks of cheery birds spring out of the figs and take to their wings. Abbu's body bends over me, cupping my face with its warm flapping leaves. Bachoo and Abbu and I whistle with the breeze and push deeper into the soil, the soil rich with water and fertilised by love.

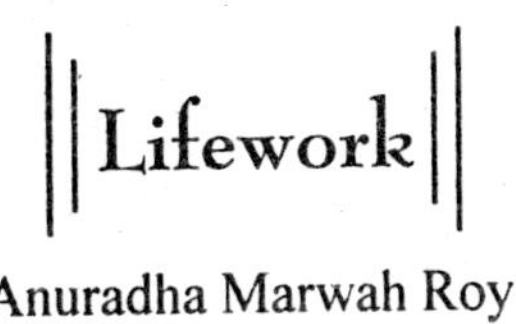

Lifework

Anuradha Marwah Roy

Mrs. Mukhopadhyaya switched on the light to peer at her watch. The thick hand was quite far from six. Too early! The time was probably a few minutes past five. Now where were her glasses? She rummaged around her pillow, shivering a little. She got out of bed and turned off the air-conditioner. The glasses were sitting on a table nearby. Why on earth had she kept them there? As soon as she put them on, blurred lines sharpened and her day began.

It was only a quarter to five. Nobody else would be stirring yet. There were expensive arrangements in this house to preserve sleep till the sun was overhead. Even if the power supply faltered which was fairly often in this colony of too many air-conditioners, noisy, pollution-spreading generators would come on to keep them spewing cool air. In the villages of this country, on the other hand ... None of her business, really! She wanted her morning tea. Could she dare to make tea in her daughter's house? Stir the hornet's nest?

"Mama, how often have I told you not to tire yourself? Don't you realise you are getting on? Why couldn't you ring for Ramlal?" Mikki would scold.

Mrs. Mukhopadhyaya would then feel constrained to point out that Ramlal, the cook, was as old if not older than her and had only gone to bed an hour after she had turned in. And of course, her mother championing the cause of the underdog would be a flaming red rag to Mikki's upper-class bull.

Mrs. Mukhopadhyaya wanted no arguments today, her special day. Today of all days, she didn't want her daughter to look at her with exasperation and say, "Oh Mama!" as though dealing with an old, cussed harridan.

Mrs. Mukhopadhyaya made the tea nevertheless, missing her late husband's elan. Throughout their twenty-six years together he was the one who had begun the morning chores, she had been – as he used to put it – the lady of the (k)night. She used to surface after he had filled the buckets in the bathroom, made tea and poured her two efficient cups, and more often than not, added to their fund of jokes about her reluctance to wake up. Now she woke many times at night. These days it was such a relief when day broke. Finishing her tea, Mrs. Mukhopadhyaya found herself carefully rinsing out her cup, and the teapot. She even emptied the electric kettle to hide all evidence of her foray into the kitchen. Slightly amused at her pusillanimity, she padded out into the garden.

It was breezy and cool. She kicked off her slippers to feel the dew on her soles. She started walking purposefully, up and down, up and down the lawn. She could feel the edges of her sari getting wet. If Jnandeb were here, he would have teased, "Your sari, Mahasveta! Must you try and sweep away the dirt everywhere?" He knew how prudish she was. He knew she would rather take on extra washing than hitch up her sari and let her calves show. Her legs were startlingly white in comparison with her sunburned arms, neck and face. He was the only one who had known her buttery smoothness. "Greta Garbo!"

"Kothai chore galo re?" she asked the gaudy red and pink bougainvillea that was nodding in the breeze, as his absence smote her like physical pain, "Why did you go away by yourself?" Lately she had taken to talking aloud to her dead husband. It comforted her. Today there was a lot to say. She was going to be felicitated by no other than the President of India. This is why she was in the capital, in their daughter's home. Their 'selfless service to society' was going to be rewarded.

"I have finished for you," she said to him. "I know awards don't mean much but this one means we've done it. It also means I was right in rescuing you from your *mashi-pishis* in Allahabad. I was right in dragging you away from *addabaazi* at the collapsing University. You were meant to educate people and that's what we did – you and I – in our unknown hamlet. We have put it on the national map: Karera, Rajasthan, where every child goes to school. I have finished your lifework for you."

Mrs. Mukhopadhyaya walked faster. She was a stately woman with waist length hair that she bunched impatiently into a bun several times a day. Her face was small, her eyes very dark and flashing. People had always turned to stare at her.

"I know you missed Shona-di's *dohi-maach* throughout," she accused her late husband, playfully. "But you'll have to admit I became quite good at cooking fish myself - not that we could get it too often. And I know you were very happy with me – far happier than you would have been with that *naika-moni* Shona-di wanted you to marry. She always blamed me – the Calcutta-girl – for spiriting you away. Now, after this public recognition of our achievement would she still say I dragged you down?"

Theirs had been a whirlwind romance followed by a marriage that left both the parental families feeling indignant. Before the relatives could recover from the shock of the precipitate marriage, the newly-weds announced their decision to leave for Karera. A new chapter began in their life then. They started their work with the underprivileged. Mrs. Mukhopadhyaya initiated it as she began everything they did together. And after a few good-natured protests about being buried alive by a sandstorm, Jnandeb allowed himself to be sucked into the large sensuous space of her creativity. The gates of their intimate world clanged shut at that point. Disapproving relatives found themselves excluded, disregarded. She conceived plans, he wrote them out as proposals developing, amending and getting them passed through crusty bureaucratic procedures. Those were heady times. Together they were converting ideals of their youth into projects. Later, Jnandeb began to express the wish to reconnect with the extended family. But with an intuitive fear of other claims, and perhaps an unacknowledged resentment of their earlier rejection of her, Mrs Mukhopadhyaya resolutely kept the door shut. All in all, there had been two bald patches in the tussocky comfort of their marital life: Jnandeb's relatives, and their daughter Mikki.

Mrs. Mukhopadhyaya had named her only daughter Shubhangi but Mikki spent all her growing years resisting that name and everything else that her mother tried to give her. What a spitfire she had been!

"Mama, why can't I go to Geeta's dance party? Why? Why? Why?"

"Mikki, it takes two hours to reach the city. How will you come back? And I don't like the idea of you staying there overnight."

"This place is a sinkhole. What should I do now that the exams are over?"

"I would love to have you over for the school-festival tomorrow, Mikki. There will be dancing too."

'You must be joking, Mama – You want me to dance with the village-women in their stinky *lehengas*?"

"Yes, I don't see what's wrong with participating in their dances."

"I hate you, Mama. I'm sure it is only because you don't want me to ever have fun. I hate you."

Mrs. Mukhopadhyaya hadn't known how to deal with her, neither had Jnandeb. It was as though their daughter grew up to speak a foreign language. She travelled two hours to school and then college everyday and it seemed that her real home was in the city, away from her parents. Mikki was very bright and very contrary. At times they wondered what would become of her. That she would end up as a docile daughter-in-law and a loving wife in a big family home, was a thought that couldn't have been further from their minds.

The news that Mikki wanted to marry Ajay had come as a shock to both her parents. After having met Ajay precisely ten times at Geeta's house – he was Geeta's cousin – Mikki had dropped the bombshell, "Yes, I am going to marry Ajay. He is rich, comes from a good family..."

Mrs. Mukhopadhyaya had dismissed all these virtues rather impatiently, "Oh yes, he is rich. But Mikki is that enough? He isn't even a graduate."

"And how will a degree help in his export business?"

"You know I am not talking about his business. I thought you wanted to train as a psychologist. Now you want to marry even before your Masters."

"I can still do it."

"What about the scholarships you said you would apply for?"

"I can study in Delhi. And I will be going abroad often enough. We are going to Switzerland for our honeymoon."

Ajay was handsome and mild-mannered. He dressed extravagantly: designer jackets and jeans. In vain, Mrs. Mukhopadhyaya tried to explain to Mikki that he belonged to the other side: the selfish, complacent upper class they had been fighting all these years. How could a Mukhopadhyaya ever adjust to their ways? But Jnandeb had been very quiet. He even exhorted her to leave Mikki alone.

"Perhaps you were right about Mikki, Mrs. Mukhopadhyaya conceded still walking like a woman possessed. "She seems exceptionally well adjusted. She has recently been elected president of a ladies club called Inner Circle. What a name: Inner Circle!"

She stopped short. She sounded condescending even to herself. Jnandeb had once said to her, "Mahasveta, you must learn to respect people who are different from you. You can't go through life being dismissive of everybody." Had there then been too much self-righteousness in her disapproval of the match? Ajay was essentially good-hearted. When Jnandeb died he had stood by her, more like a son than son-in-law. He had been the only one to understand her need to lose control. While others concentrated on shushing her, he alone offered his shoulder, "Cry, Mummy. Don't bottle it up." She had collapsed thankfully and wept for hours. He had also taken over the arrangements for the funeral.

Later on, his expressions of grief started to irritate her, "Mummy, I can't let you stay alone. What will you do in this place?"

"I have my work, our school. How can I leave it now that he's gone?"

"No, no! You must move in with us. Our house is big enough. There's no need for you to work now."

The need to work! Couldn't he understand it was work that needed her, pulling at her hem like a child. The grant from Norway had not come through then. It was only now after she had utilised it to start free computer classes in the school that she could think of retiring – although not in the way Mikki and Ajay meant.

She sighed! No matter how she put it to herself, Mikki had let them down. "You wouldn't have liked these things either," she said sadly to Jnandeb's absence. "Mikki has grown too far from us. You and I were different right from the beginning. We married at that time without the usual pageantry. I didn't even wear the customary 'loha'. People called me a witch. But we never bowed to social pressure. Even now, I never wear that horrible stark white," Mrs. Mukhopadhyaya said, gulping painfully.

"And Mikki!" She continued, complaining in real earnest, "She seems to bend backwards for social approval. Remember her wedding reception! Remember the food, the kind of people, the empty talk! She's become just like them. It's as though she was never our child!"

Marriage had transformed Mikki: she wore single diamonds – solitaires – in her ears, and diamond rings that sparkled like little lights on her fingers. She hosted parties, yelled at her servants, and shopped compulsively. She had of course already touched the nadir of ostentatiousness much before – when Mrs. Mukhopadhyaya saw her wearing a seven string diamond necklace. But in spite of her, Mrs. Mukhopadhyaya had been unable to stifle a gasp at the stars around Mikki's white neck. Dressed in pink, Mikki had seemed like a princess that evening. At the five-star reception hosted by Ajay's parents, in stark contrast to the Spartan wedding at the Mukhopadhyayas, Mrs. Mukhopadhyaya had been dumbstruck for a while. Perhaps for the first time in her life, she had caressed gems and doubted herself. Her lovely daughter! What right had she to have kept her in rags and soot?

Both she and Jnandeb had been tearful and contrite. Had they actually given their daughter nothing? How would Mikki's in-laws respond to the meanness of her origins? Would they cherish her ultimately or would they always be condescending: dressing her up in their expensive clothes, embellishing her with their jewellery?

But that mood had passed quickly with the evening. That mood passed when they saw the obscene quantity of food on the dinner table. Outside the hotel they had already spotted two shrivelled urchins scratching at car windows, selling mogra garlands for one rupee apiece. Mrs. Mukhopadhyaya, her heart melting with tenderness, had bought ten. So, by the time Mikki and Ajay came to them for *aashirvad*, tears had dried up in their eyes. They had been unable to share Mikki's enthusiasm for the bridal suite (with compliments from the hotel) and the honeymoon trip to Switzerland (a present from her in-laws). In fact they had left Delhi precipitately the very next day. Safely ensconced in their village home, they had distributed *laddoos* among the school children. Jnandeb had sighed, "She seemed happy. That's all we should ask for." Then together they had relinquished their daughter – making a mental *kanyadan* which was far crueller than the ritual they had refused to perform.

Letters kept plying between mother and daughter but they were stiff little notes. Are you well? Yes I'm well. How is Ajay's business doing? We have bought a new car, a Honda Accord this time. The Governor came to the school, state scholarships for three children. Mama, I am pregnant. Hope you are eating well.

"She'll even bear her children according to their wishes. No doubt there will be a second pregnancy soon. Her mother-in-law was saying it's high time," grumbled Mrs. Mukhopadhyaya. It was getting warm but she was unmindful of the perspiration dripping down her neck.

Soon after Mikki's delivery, Mrs. Mukhopadhyaya had travelled to Delhi bearing gifts for Ajay's family – silk kurtas and Daccai saris, spending far more than she ever had on clothes. These were peace offerings, bought with mutual consent. Jnandeb and she were excited at the idea of a grandchild of their own.

So extravagant had she been that Ajay's mother protested, "Why are you spending so much? Such gifts are given only when a boy is born. You are not expected to do all this for a girl."

Bristling with indignation, Mrs. Mukhopadhyaya had looked at Ajay and Mikki hoping for a retort. None came. Beautiful Mikki wore a bovine expression. In the exclusive nursing home the labour had been long and tedious, ultimately resulting in a Caesarian section. Throughout her one month stay Mrs. Mukhopadhyaya tried several ways to get through to her daughter but perhaps she had left it too late. Mikki was impatient, rejecting outright her mother's suggestion that she enrol for a course at the Open University, and use the years of parenting that would keep her home, gainfully. "I have no intention of retiring from active partying, Mama," she replied scornfully.

However, Mrs. Mukhopadhyaya found it impossible to overlook the conventional gifts of fortune in Mikki's life – there seemed to be many. Although it was 'only a girl', Ajay and his parents regaled the mother and child with their brand of care and concern. Ajay's mother climbed three flights of stairs to buy a special crib-mobile – a feat that was exclaimed at by everyone who knew how difficult it was for her to even walk. A nurse was hired to look after the baby at night, as Mikki was 'too weak', this was in addition to the ayah who was there all day. When Mrs. Mukhopadhyaya came to know what was being spent and offered to do the night shift, Ajay was indignant to the point of being rude.

Strangely, Mrs. Mukhopadhyaya found that she could talk more easily with Ajay's family than with her own daughter. She would tell the plump, good-natured couple about the desert, the feuds fought over a bucket of water, the gruelling poverty. They listened with distracted admiration. That admiration became focussed when Ajay saw the Minister of Education at his father-in-law's funeral; now with the national award Mikki's marital family was eager to co-opt her as their own. Mrs. Mukhopadhyaya had been welcomed far in more warmly this time than she ever had before. No doubt, they would say at their innumerable parties – Mikki's parents, you know, the well-known social workers ....

Perhaps the achievement of this acceptance had also been a part of their work. Mrs. Mukhopadhyaya smiled somewhat mockingly: "Mikki's at last got what she wanted – high-powered parents!"

She felt a heady sense of release. She had made her peace, even with Mikki. Now perhaps the time had come at last to close her eyes and cease. After Jnandeb, it had become very difficult to carry on from day to day. She was very, very tired. It was Mrs. Mukhopadhyaya's unshakable belief that death would be hers for the asking, as life had always been. She would switch off the light by which she worked and it would be pitch dark. She did not admit twilight to her scheme of things.

"Shuncho, it's all taken care of. I can come too," she said aloud like a young wife. eager to wind up and join her husband for a holiday.

Suddenly there was a sound behind her. It was Mikki.

"Mama, are you mad? What are you doing walking around in the heat and muttering to yourself?"

Mrs. Mukhopadhyaya allowed herself to be ushered indoors. Seated in Mikki's bedroom, she noticed that her daughter's eyes were swollen and red.

"You really are the limit, Mama..." Mikki was saying.

"Mikki, what happened? Have you been crying?"

"Mama, I am pregnant..."

"Oh! Where is Ajay?"

"Out."

"So early?"

Mikki did not reply.

"Why have you been crying Mikki?"

"I ... no ... don't ..."

"What is it? You might have a son this time. Everybody in your family has been waiting for this."

"I don't want to have another child."

"Have you spoken to Ajay?"

"He says he will take me for an amniocentesis, if it is a girl I can have it aborted ..."

"What if it is a boy?" asked Mrs. Mukhopadhyaya sharply.

"Then, I will have to go through with it. Mama, I nearly died with the first one, I don't want another..."

"You didn't nearly die with the first one. You had the best possible medical attention and then no two deliveries are the same."

Mikki broke down. Loud sobs racked her body, "Is this all you can say? Is this all anybody can ever say to me, look at how much you have, count your blessings, count your diamonds, your cars. I am sick of this Mama, I can't, I won't give them a son in return. I won't go through the whole thing again."

Mrs. Mukhopadhyaya sat stunned. Mikki hadn't ever cried like this before. Never!

"Why don't you tell Ajay you don't want another child?"

"It's no use. He just parrots his mother."

"Mikki, that's not being fair. Your in-laws are decent people."

"So, what should I do? Become a child-bearing machine in return?"

"You can refuse to have the baby."

"I don't know ... I don't know ... I wish I hadn't been pushed into this..."

"Pushed? Pushed into what?"

"Into this mess...into this marriage..."

"What do you mean? You married Ajay by choice."

Mikki reared up from the bed, "Choice? What choice did I have? I hated the way we lived – dingy, horrible, hot. And you didn't let me do anything I wanted. I didn't want to study further but there you were pushing me for all you were worth. I just said once in passing that I like psychology and you had my future chalked out as a Clinical Psychologist with a degree from – from – God knows where!"

Mikki ranted on. "Did you ever try to find out what I really wanted? I didn't want laurels and awards, I wanted to have fun. I hated your principles, your negation."

"My what?"

"Your negation. No new clothes for puja because it was against your principles, no jewellery because it was against your principles, no parties because you had no time, only talk, talk, talk with people in shabby clothes..."

Mikki sobbed and sobbed, "I didn't want to be you. I didn't want to look like you – so eccentric. And you kept pushing me, pushing me. If I hadn't married Ajay, you would have got what you wanted – a clone."

Mrs. Mukhopadhyaya sat immobile, a statue. Thoughts were whirling too fast inside. Fun? So, you've had your fun. Do you know the price you paid to enter the circus? Was it worth it Mikki? But she didn't say a word. She had just realised the price she would have to pay in order to say this. Just when she was putting down her tools her daughter had returned scorched with her own fire. Work at rebuilding a life was pulling at Mrs. Mukhopadhyaya's hem again.

With a hand at the end of an arm that seemed to weigh a ton, she reached out to push back Mikki's hair from her forehead, "What do you want Mikki?"

"I don't know," said her daughter taken aback by her mother's gentleness.

"Then I – we'll have to find out, won't we?""

Mikki was silent.

"Shubhangi, my daughter, will you come home with me?"

Mikki looked up surprised, "For what?"

"You can take back Baba's reward to the school."

"I can't be away for too long," Mikki replied reluctantly.

Mrs. Mukhopadhyaya put her arms around her daughter. They sat with scarcely a movement, three generations locked together. After a while, Mrs. Mukhopadhyaya's eyes rose to the window, "A last-minute emergency. But I'll set her right in no time," she said silently to the bougainvillea.

A Toast to Herself

Raji Narasimhan

Shall we see Dr. Kesavan one of these days?"

Priya looks up blinking. Time has a way of splintering and colliding in this house. Kesavan is a suitor of hers. An undeclared one, the kind that goes out of sight for years together and then shows up one day with the same desires, frisking his eyes.

"Yes, of course, mother," she says quickly, to still the squall gone up in her. She is expecting a review of her latest book in the papers. The suspense and its symptoms are familiar: a muted whistling like the inside of a telephone, in her stomach, and criss-crossing her head, a throbbing. Joshi of the *Herald* has told her he'll be publishing it soon. Soon means now, the swollen present, holding time in its maw. Her fifth book. She measures her age against her books and her writing career. Tall in their book-case, her books assure her that she is fifty years young. But fifty vanishes when she sets it against her flirtation with Kesavan. She becomes twenty then, the years when she thought about independence a lot and always found it leading her by the nose into a sexual muddle. And when it comes to her mother, when she acts her fifty years of experience and pain against her mother's crumbling frame and still doughty eyes, she becomes the baffling woman, perennial and beyond age.

"Good. Let's hear what Kesavan has to say about this bag of stale blood." Her mother points at herself, laughing, and turns to go into the kitchen with a sudden spurt of energy.

Alone in the verandah, under the dense vines, Priya tosses to collect herself. She wants to think coolly about the coming review, and see for herself the spartan and committed writing person she knows herself to be. But her thoughts slip to Kesavan. Sex always lurks in some fold of her mind, vying with writing for the possession of her.

Years ago, Kesavan had called her into his clinic when he need not have, and had given her an injection in her buttock.

"A precaution, no more," he had said, looking through semi-closed eyes at the raised hump of her posterior. He explained that there was a virus raging in the air: She had accepted his explanation. She was far too miserable, what with her divorce, her mother's active and open hatred of her for it, her joblessness, and her mother's active and open hatred of her for *that,* her youth, her insecurity.

"It won't pain," Kesavan poised the syringe above her rump. "And when are you going back to your husband?" his voice glided smoothly to the question.

Her answer came just before the needle's plunge. "I'm not going back."

The sharp pain of the needle stung and subsided.

He kept his eyes averted when she sat opposite him at his desk and he passed his prescription slip towards her. "It is going to be difficult for you," he said, still looking away. Minutes passed. He seemed about to make a proposal. She might even have accepted him. But he didn't. All his natural caution exerted its weight against his urge to speak out. The minutes passed on. He made no proposal. It was clear that he wasn't going to make any.

And then what happened?

The sequence fades in Priya's mind. She rubs her eyes. There are dark half-moons under them, she sees, without having to look in the mirror. And she feels, without touching, the roughened, coarsened skin on the moons. The knowledge of ugliness puts her back in tune with herself as a writer. She stands up, hardy and striving. Should she telephone Joshi and ask him carefully, casually about the review?

But her mother is back, standing before her.

"Not at work yet, I see." She's not really being sarcastic about her incomeless work. Only, she still finds it necessary to state these queer things about her It's her way of finally accepting their queerness.

Priya gives the bright, watchful smile she gives whenever these asides begin with her mother.

"I'm a useless old body, aren't I?" her mother hovers close for a near look at her daughter who could seem like a stranger for all the fights they'd had. "Uneducated, unfit for anything except brewing *rasam* and *sambar*. What is it you are writing now?

Story? Article? Why should you tell me? Will I understand?"

"If I were not your daughter, mother, you would. You would even like what I write," Priya laughs to sound sporting.

Her mother laughs too, reading Priya's afterthought.

"Tell me, they pay you well now, don't they? They pay you a decent amount for your efforts, don't they?"

"You know very well, they don't. Two hundred, two fifty is the most I get for an item."

"But you do four items a month, you must be! Writing all the time! A thousand you make then!"

"A taxi driver makes more!"

Her mother closes up under the sudden rasp of Priya's voice. Priya laughs to soften the outburst. But she's driven to more. "And I'll remain poor. You know that as much as me. So stop your make-believe."

Her mother is silenced. She's too old to snap back and bandy words. But as always she's succeeded in stirring awake the fear of poverty latent in both of them. Priya keeps a stiff face. She will not rise to the bait. She will not let her mother get away with her tricks.

Her mother recedes into herself. Priya knows exactly how she will spend the afternoon. She will stand pressed to the gate looking out for the postman to bring her her widow's pension for the month. It isn't due yet. The month isn't over yet. But she will still stand there glued to the gate, forgetting to eat.

"Come back, mother. It is not the first yet. You won't be getting it," Priya will call. And her mother will answer without taking her eyes off the road. "Last time he brought it on the twenty-sixth."

Priya sighs. How often has she assured her mother: "Your money is your own, mother. I want none of it. I can fend for myself."

"You'll live like a *sanyaasini,* then? Your writing brings you pebbles."

"But I want little, mother. I don't want much, honestly. I can never make you understand. I don't understand it myself."

She really doesn't. Her wants have shrunk suddenly ever since she went into writing. The substance rising and forming within her seems too fine for the normal plenitudes. It seems to want tending most of all, tending that consists of intensive communication with the eyes and turns of voice, and encouraging gestures with the hands without close touching. It keeps her cheerful even when hunger charges into her and chaps her lips and a crumpled *kurta* pulled out of the dhobi's basket makes up her clothing.

The pension money has bloated her mother's savings. She isn't sure, but it would be sixty, or seventy thousand at least. Sitting under the thick vines, wracked with anxiety about the review, the face of Kesavan prying in and out in a degenerate sexual recall, Priya slides off to a calculation of her mother's assets. Seven hundred and fifty rupees a month in the bank for eight years. Amounts to seventy-two thousand rupees. Seventy-two thousand.

In ten lives she wouldn't see such a sum.

"You must be thinking me a greedy old crone," her mother flits around her table sometimes, watching her intent writing look with jealous scrutiny and smudging it wantonly, boldly.

"What do you want me to say, mother?" Priya snaps, her brows unlocking under the impact. "I will not play Mother Comfort! Enjoy your guilt yourself!"

It's lulling under the vines. Priya disengages herself from its protective warmth and goes to telephone Joshi. How much should she have to put a stop to this insidious tribute to money her mother forces out of her? She is thinking this out as she walks to the phone. Against her mother's seventy-two thousand how much will she need as fortification against these maraudings into her privacy?

Joshi's number is engaged. She tries again. Still engaged. The downward beeps of the engaged signal carry her down with them to memories of Kesavan.

Her next memorable meeting with him was in the flush of her wrestles with her first novel. He'd been sent for by his mother.

"Why have I sent for you, doctor?" Her mother had lain back stagily in her chair, pressing the all too true, far from sham pains in her heart. "What does it matter if this rickety heart stops?"

Tut-tutting and cluck-clucking, composing her with his competent medical hands, he had fixed inquiring and accusing eyes on Priya. He didn't need to ask if she'd joined her husband. Her defensive and hostile eyes told him all. She hadn't aged unduly, he hadn't failed to notice. He smiled in spite of himself.

"What are you doing these days?" He was playfully possessive.

"Writing!" Her mother snapped.

"Stories etcetera?" Layman's curiosity shone in his eyes.

"Sort of," she smiled formally.

"Why don't you let me see them?"

The dumbkopf would never have known what to make of them. He didn't really know English even though he spoke it. She was afraid, suddenly. What if he quizzed her? What if he got out of her all those little secrets about writing that formed from the duplicities of making art from life?

Kesavan saw her fidgeting. It revived his own inhibitions, and at the same time his sympathies. Priya felt herself go woman and winding like a mermaid. She would have liked to rest her head on his chest and take the male comfort she had rejected all these years. She wished she could take a respite from the exacting taskmaster of writing to which she had bound herself.

"Tell her, doctor," her mother wailed, face turned full to him, and in sharp profile to her. "Explain to her that writing is for those with money. For those like her, it is a hobby only. Explain that to her, doctor, make her understand."

Joshi's number is still engaged. In the waiting for the line to clear, her anxiety about the review mounts. What is a review? Just words. One more noise among many. "Will you stop writing if this review doesn't appear?" she asks herself sternly, and hears herself whine. "Yes, I might." "Yes, you might," the pronoun changes as she addresses herself, linking up with her ventriloquist's voice. "Something will break in me." "Something will break in you," the pronouns clash. She moves away from the telephone, needing distance and space. From the balcony she sees her mother down below shuffling about the patch of grass. Later in the afternoon, at four thirty, she's able to contact Joshi. "It's coming this week," Joshi sounds light-hearted. The pages must have been made up and put to bed.

Now the fear is close and biting like a mask. Her movements retract inwards, stiff jointed. Twice in the night she wakes up and tries to push away the boa's fangs of fear.

In the morning the paper is on the porch. The judgement on her lies in its folds. Under stress Priya's reading becomes a crab-like backward and forward movement. She alights somewhere in the middle of a sentence, goes up a little and then skims down, picking out words that seem key and leading. "Sensitive," she picks out. A cliche, but encouraging. "Imbued with life," she takes in and winds back quickly to the head of the sentence. "Characters are," is the head. She smiles severely. Cliche, cliche. Who is the reviewer? The name is vaguely familiar. "A welcome addition to the growing body of ..." Shut up, shut up, shut up, she grimaces in pleasure and disgust. Well, it's a nice review. Flattering even. Elation possesses her. She lets herself be possessed by it before good sense and anticlimax catch up.

It is night. A navy blue sky lies looped above. Priya, Kesavan and her mother are on the lawn, sipping lemonade. The doctor is tearing the skin of the night to see her face. He has seen it already. It wasn't dark when he came, and he has seen the still presentable face and form of her. But he wants to see them again to make sure. His fluttery voice sails up to her in the dark. "So you've become a big writer. I saw a review of your book in the paper today."

Priya pauses before the next sip of her lemonade. She doesn't think it necessary to reply to him. She gives a polite laugh. She can feel the doctor's smile and attention hammering her. She lets them hammer her on.

"How much royalty has she got? Ask her that! She has got nothing! Tell me if I am wrong!" Her mother may not sound bitter about her poverty, but she's insulting all right under her open manner.

The doctor is confused as usual. "Money isn't everything, Amma," he murmurs. And then he turns to Priya, suddenly aggressive.

"Why don't you let me see all that you've written these years? Why are you still hiding them from me?"

"Very well! I shan't hide them!"

Her response catches them unawares. Gliding along the cool grass she goes in and comes back with a full set of her books. She puts them on the table.

"There, that's the lot."

She steps away from them and in the dark sees them huddled like children separated from their mother. Wrapped in their jackets, they do seem like her physical offsprings, sprung from the clay and kiln of her body.

The doctor picks up the ones on top, feeling their girth and shape. "They're all yours?" he asks in wonder.

"They are," Priya laughs.

He picks them up one after the other, till they are spread in both his hands. His hands become heavy and populous with them. For many seconds he stands thus, laden. Then he begins to put the books back on the table, offloading them like prize cargo. "I will read them," he says solemnly as if taking a vow.

He never will, Priya knows. They're not popular reading. And her English, made heightened and subjective, will be a sore trial to him.

Her mother has melted too. "Haven't you really made even a paisa from them all, Priya? For all the hours you've spent on them, not a paisa you've made."

Tomorrow she might well change. Tomorrow in the clear light of day her mother might well not be any more the kindly person she is now. But tomorrow a lot of things might well change. Kesavan's growing up may no longer mean anything. The review will certainly fade into the irrelevance it is. Tomorrow she will be again at her game of worming into herself and seeing what she has come up with. But that's tomorrow. Today she will joke with the doctor. She will laugh with her mother. She will drink lemonade. She will forget and drink a toast to herself.

Recollecting Motherhood

Mrinal Pande

A close, reading of women's writings from the *Therigatha* (The Songs of Buddhist Nuns), to Mahasweta Devi's and Ambai's fiction reveals that motherhood as women truly experience it and motherhood as a much glorified institution are as separate and distinct from each other, as Gandhiji is from Gandhianism. As an institution, motherhood comes to young women, as an already perfected idea, a system built by a patriarchal society. And when the family elders bless them and say "may you be the mother of many sons", it has all the heaped force of custom and tradition, behind it. Actual motherhood as women experience it, however, is an immensely personal and intense experience, that fuses mind and body as nothing also can.

On the surface many things have been changing for our women since Independence, including the concept of motherhood. By the

1970s, a young woman from a liberal urban middle-class family could enter college, move around the campus with boyfriends; postpone marriage till she had rounded off her studies well, and then postpone child bearing for sometime till it was convenient to have a baby. But now, when one thinks about those years, even then those seemingly wider choices were strictly limited. One had the choice for example, to study further and (having armed oneself with a degree), to compete in an economic system with confidence. But you could do it, only if the men of your family (read father, father-in-law, husband) permitted you to do so. One of the routine questions asked at job interviews of women remained: Do you have your father's permission?

Once you got married, motherhood as an institution took over. Even the most liberal families conveyed to you (through mother, older sisters, mothers-in-law) that they would now like to see you "settle down", with a baby, hopefully a boy, to carry on the line. Neither the women go-betweens nor the glossy magazines and books, that they left suggestively for the young woman in question, spoke to her about a young wife's own feelings of conflict, her problems with a sudden loss of her name, her identity, and of the freedom to work at her own pace. All well-bred young women, whether working or not, were supposed to integrate themselves unquestioningly into the unchanging, age-old social structures, that had made it impossible for their well-educated mothers and aunts to have independent careers, and develop as individuals. It was a situation tailor-made for rebellion. Men too married around the same age, yet fatherhood was not expected to become their full-time vocation, at the cost of their job. Why should a woman's reproductive role then subsume her productive one? But when one raised such obvious questions, it was as though one was talking in an obsolete tongue. At best it was: "She will get out of it by and by" and at worst: "How dare she? Was this why we brought her into the family, that instead of producing sons, she should leave home each day to go out and work?"

The 1975 report on the status of women made it clear how for the poorest (i.e. three-quarters) of women, things were terribly grim, and that the thought that women are intrinsically as human as men was simply unavailable to our planners and policy-makers. But what went largely unreported was how things were hardly better for the women from the so-called privileged classes. There was a reason for this. Almost all our movers and shakers were upper caste men from the upper classes. And in most cases even in the families of our top politicians, bureaucrats and industrialists, women were being idealised and exploited at the same time in the name of tradition and motherhood. One met and heard these women at social-dos and formal official get-togethers quite frequently, and saw how in order to survive and to win social approval, most of them had accepted the traditional concept of motherhood, where being a wife and mother was being a person with no need for a further identity. As the wife and the mother, they lived at others' pace, fitting all their needs and energies to groom and protect them. They were all uniformly isolated and somewhat bored, but what the hell, this was a glorious sacrifice. A virtue that was its own reward. No one took notice if some of them talked to friends about experiencing baby-blues, and uncontrollable rages that ended in migraine and hysteria.

Nor did one open one's mouth about the stress of being made solely responsible for the children and the near-total lack of privacy, self-esteem and sleep it entailed. Most seemed to accept this unfair stereotype as a woman's biological *karma*. If women spoke of occasional bursts of a murderous anger when husbands took to keeping crazy work-schedules and children became too noisy or disobedient, it was treated as a joke. If they left the children at all, to meet friends or see a movie, the young mothers were made to suffer pangs of terminal guilt for this dereliction of maternal duties. They hardly ever remembered what they saw or read or discussed while they were away from their maternal watch towers. Most confessed they had forgotten when they last read a whole book or even skimmed through newspapers.

But some did not give up. They were trying to go beyond, as they struggled to bring back their own intellectual lives into focus. At the staff-rooms of the various universities - where I taught, and later among young women journalists, I was overwhelmed by a discovery of wonderfully vibrant minds that traditional maternity had failed to subserviate. Between discussing literary criticism and contemporary political situations, these women talked freely of their lives as a working mother, who was suspect in all eyes, including her own. Of how annoying it was to want to be human,and be told you must be a mother first. They saw nothing wrong abut complaining freely about those ridiculous family-dos and parties at which men formed tight little Freemasonic clubs and talked of the Future of India, while women with minds and vocations of their own, were made to sit in little giggly clusters and were lectured to by supercilious and dismissive matrons, who had dedicated their own lives to their children's welfare and their husband's careers.

Slowly the anger dissipated and the working women of the 1980s rediscovered their lost sense of humour.

They then laughed about mothers and mothers-in-law who bustled about to get a cup of hot tea for those terminally fatigued men at the end of the day, and they laughed at how they darted poisonous glances at their equally tired working daughters and daughters-in-law and made nasty wisecracks about those who succumbed to selfishness, pride and avarice and predicted that working women would break up the happy homes they had built.

But this was a very long journey.

Once in a while fellow-writers say this to many of us: why do you limit yourself to "soft issues", and travel so much to rural areas to report on women? Why not write more about contemporary (read male) politics, about the process of democratisation? If you must, why not write about motherhood as a positive influence that has shaped your own personality? Look at the men. They do not complain. Their bonds with their mothers, and wives, daughters, their girl-friends are so positive and have produced such literary gems. How is it that you do not say how it is the supportive family man who allowed you to be what you are? Come on, give credit where it is due!

After some some 30 odd years, I think I can answer this. It is like this. Before you can recollect the past creatively, you need to experience a certain tranquillity of soul. Men have no idea how rarely women get to savour it while they raise families. And it was exactly in search of that tranquillity that I absented myself from traditional mothering and entered the world of writing. It became to me, as to countless others like me, a fabled room of my own where I regained my lost identity. And it was not as though children did not matter or were shut out totally. Even as one wrote, one still had to uproot oneself frequently to answer their needs. Also answer the door, the phone, to do a car-pool turn, or the laundry; or help with a school project or keep sick-bed vigil. But through all the tedium such chores generate, it was the writing that relieved the stress and allowed me to love my daughters, without recrimination or guile. They in turn, learnt to respect a mother's privacy. Together we survived the demanding and chaotic careers of their parents and their equally chaotic school and college lives. And in this process all became individual survivors, with minds and fulfilling lives of their own. Strong ties still continue to connect us in sickness and in health, but we do not need to resort to emotional blackmail or spectacular tantrums to get attention or to tie each other down. My generation of working women has taught me, that we have no reason not to express our feelings out loud and clear, sometimes even in violent tones. That unless we take ourselves seriously, no one else will. Tapping ancient lore has told us how we can be both the calm Saraswati and angry Kali, the benign Lakshmi or the matricidal Matrikas. And this is what motherhood ultimately is: a swirling blend of pain and pleasure, frustration and fulfilment, angry resentment and pure unalloyed love. This is the motherhood tradition mostly chose to censor in our lives. And, of course, it has never been mentioned in (largely male-written) formal histories, where fatherhood alone means legitimacy and motherhood remains a tightly controlled and guarded area, where once a mother always a mother.

But how little we have heard of what happens after the progeny has flown the coop, and the uterus has called it a day. This truth is one that history has ignored, which women have refused to acknowledge, and which fellow poetesses and seers among women, from Kashmir to Kanyakumari, have recorded:

"... Wherever my son is I do not know.
This is the womb that carried him,
Like a stone cave
Lived in a by a tiger and now abandoned.
It is on the battlefield that you will find him.

Kavar Pentu

I died for no one, O Shiva, and none shall die for me.
Look within Laldyad, my Guru said, to me,
And I, Laldyad, began to wander
Unrestrained."

Laldyad's Vakh

It is out of these wanderings that great literature of the 21st century will be born.

The Rooster and the Hen

Sujata Sankranti

After months of scouting and hunting I came up on the house. It was tucked away behind one of those busy important roads of the city. A cool, high ceilinged bungalow surrounded by shady trees and an ill-kempt garden, a walking distance from my work place. Straight from the Registrar's office we drove down to the house. Malini's and my parents were too willing to set us up in a plush flat in a posh locality. But we would hear none of it. It didn't matter; we had only a big bath-attached room and a strip of a veranda at the rear portion of the building. When I gave our address as 12 Jai Singh Road, rear portion, I felt good even though it was discriminatingly demarcated – the 'rear'. After all it was our own dwelling. Father and mother said, it was heartless on my part to have rejected their plea to bring the bride home, as was the custom.

Rituals and customs, all sentimental stuff, I am sick of them.

Hollow words! Bourgeois hypocrisy! I will raise a family on different lines. Mother says I will change though. She reminds me of my 'tavarish' days. After gruelling sessions of 'self-examinations' and 'self-criticisms' with the comrades, I had gone on a rampage in Mama's beautiful garden uprooting green grass and flowering plants. Until my hands bled I had pulled at the roots which had carved a crisscross of veins under the earth. Those were the days when I had dreamt of a new earth and a new heaven in the order of Lenin and Mao. As a fifteen-year-old hardcore activist I wanted to replace grass and flowers with 'cabbages and cotton'. Now people quote tauntingly in my presence 'perestroika' and Tiananmen Square. Russia and China are not my conscience keepers. The leaps and falls of giants do not rattle me. I have my own convictions and visions.

A one-room dwelling! How can I cook, sleep and receive guests, in a single room? Vallabh says, cook in the veranda. That means, parading myself to the prying eyes of *dhobis*, *maalis*, and sweepers. Of course I do spend half the day staring at them simply because our home looks straight into the servant's block. That was something Vallabh had not bargained for. Perhaps he was too anxious to settle the accommodation he didn't think of the ugly rows of these one-roomed shacks, directly facing the back portion of the building. He does feel bad about it. But we cannot afford to leave the house as yet. Vallabh doesn't call these shacks servant quarters. He has christened them 'satellite' houses, I don't know why. I know, they exist on the borrowed strength of the bureaucrat, housed in the bungalow. But most of these domestic-helps have planted themselves here as permanent fixtures for decades. Basanti, the sweeper tells me, the old tailor staying in one of the quarters has been here for the past four decades. As a young man he had stitched shirts and smocked gowns for the British family, which had lived here during colonial times. Babujis come and go once in three or four years, but the *dhobis* and sweepers are here to stay.

Finally I decided to design the kitchen in the bedroom itself. I divided the big room with a decorative screen into two neat sections – a kitchen corner and a cosy sleeping-shrine. A table lamp by the side of the bed and a brass flower vase – the room now looked pleasant enough. I knew Vallabh would frown at me. He wanted a place to live, he said, not a museum for displaying acquisitions.

He wanted me to make only functional arrangements; he always reminded me, aesthetics should not be our priority. Yet when I turned the veranda which had a flimsy *jafery* door, painted in a cool shade of green into a mini sitting room Vallabh was not too unhappy. He helped me pull three huge tin trunks together. I fixed a few padded cushions on them and covered them with a flowery sheet and there it was – a functional seat and a beautiful settee! It is now Vallabh's favourite seat. He spends his mornings, huddled on it, his hands wrapped around the tall mug of tea, and enjoys planning his day ahead.

The new tenants at the back seem to be decent folks. The old spinster, the drawing teacher at the government school had lived here over twelve years. When Bablu's papa had brought me to the quarters as a bride, that was twelve years ago, she was there. I cleaned the room and washed clothes for her and whenever she had her rheumatic attacks I used to massage her legs and back with herbal oils. Basanti, there is magic in your hands, she used to tell me. But what a miser she was! She wouldn't give me a pie more than fifty rupees, which was the salary fixed ten years ago. The new memsaheb is young and kind. She has promised to pay me two hundred rupees. She got married only last month, she tells me. I can't believe it. She wears no jewellery, not even bangles on her wrists. No *sindoor.* No new clothes. I have never seen her in a sari. She always wears slacks and shirts like a man. I told her this would not do. If you want to keep your man you must take care of your looks. I don't know why she went into a fit of laughter.

You should have seen Basanti's face when I told her, I had brought from my parent's house neither jewellery nor any trousseau. In fact I had refused to carry with me, the utensils, the furniture, the quilts and the embroidered sheets – my mother had been hoarding for me ever since I was born. She sat down on the floor with the mopping cloth, her mouth wide open, Saheb took you without any *dahej?* And his parents? They had not demanded anything? She refused to believe. What do you think marriage is? An exchange of cattle? *Dahej!* My foot! You think I would allow my parents to buy for me a bridegroom? She wasn't prepared – and I knew it went above and beyond her head – for one of those fiery speeches, I am so used to making, at the women's development centre.

I don't like the idea of Basanti working in the house. After all a one room boarding and lodging is something Malini and I should be able to manage our selves. But Malini says Basanti is so hard up she needs money to feed her four children and her loafer husband. She is too proud to take anything free. We are only providing employment for her. Well, That is a heartening thought. But for Malini, here is an excellent opportunity. She does not have to step out of the gate to complete her project work on the *dalit* women. All the data is here, in these one-roomed shacks!

Vallabh says I am unnecessarily getting involved with Basanti. Take her up only as your case history, he tells me. But Basanti is such a dear thing. Her quarters are nearest to our veranda. So I see her every day. Her day starts at five every morning, summer or winter, rain or storm. She scrubs her brass vessels with charcoal and sand until they shine and neatly puts them away in a wire basket to dry. Then she would go straight to the night jasmine tree and shake the flower laden branches delicately scented small flowers, they have bright orange colour stems and soft pearly white petals. Usually these flowers which have only a night's life, fall off on the ground by morning, spreading under the tree a soft coral and pearl carpet. Basanti told me, the flowers fallen on the ground are not to be taken for *pooja.* So she would collect them in her *pallav.* She would tuck the flowers safely into the folds of her *pallav* and with a small bowl of milk in her hand would set out to the Shiva shrine, at the back of the house. All married women must worship Shiva, she told me once, and should do *abhishek,* bathe the *Shivaling* with milk. That was the right way to ensure long life for one's husband, she told me as though she was warning me! I wonder why she wants that brute of a husband to live long. When I see her fawning around such a useless man – simply because he has given her married status – my blood boils. For days and days he roams around the city gambling and drinking. Yet when he comes home she treats him like a king. She lays a feast to welcome him! Whenever she comes to borrow from me cloves and cinnamon I know the prodigal husband has returned. She wants to make for him chicken *khorma!* All that she had saved during the entire month, sweeping and swabbing the bungalows of Babujis, would go into that one meal. She would place the shining brass *thali* on an embroidered red scarf and place the delicacies – a mound of rice, *puris* puffed into golden domes, *daal* and curries. She would then spread a *durry* on the floor and the children would conduct him to his seat. Basanti would be sitting a few feet away and fanning – I always wondered whether she was fanning her husband or driving away flies from the *thall.* Babloo, Bittu and Guddi would squat around their father and solemnly watch him, chewing the chicken bones and smacking his lips. If he left a few pieces of chicken Bittu and Babloo would fall on them. I asked Basanti why the children were never allowed to join the feast. The man of the house must eat first and then the boys would eat; whatever is left the girls should eat. Basanti had the answer ready. As night falls, I would hear screams and yells from Basanti's quarters. The next morning I would see her limping around with her limbs beaten black and blue. And the vagabond of a husband would have once again taken to the road. Basanti takes everything as her fate, as if nothing can ever be changed. What a miserable lot! Before I leave this house I must rescue Basanti.

Padlock on the *jafery* door? I have not taken with me the

duplicate key. I never felt the need for it. Malini hardly ever goes anywhere without telling me. It is half past six, in fact an hour later than my usual time. Why am I feeling so piqued? Do I expect my wife to stand at the door straining her ears for the footsteps of her lord and master? What is happening to me? Is Basanti's idyll slowly worming its way into my mind? I must say I feel a bit envious of her loafer husband. The fellow doesn't have to raise one little finger, pampered by his wife and children, fed with delicacies; he is a real emperor in his hut. Sitting on the floor fanning him and his food, furtively, throwing at him sidelong glances; even the plain-faced portly Basanti looks charming. How would Malini look with a red *bindi* on her broad forehead, and the sari thrown over her head? Like a full moon, no like the fourteenth day moon, how can there be a day-moon? Oh, my aesthetics is all wrong. I must say lyrically, in the native way *'chaudh-vin ka chand'*.

I wanted to be back before Vallabh returns. The temple was so crowded. And Basanti insisted we should wait for the *arti.* I enjoyed the colourful crowd, the *keertan,* the bells and the flickering lamps. It was like a psychedelic dell. What a thing to say about the temple! I hardly looked at the idol. When Basanti pleaded with me to visit the temple with her I had no heart to say no. I was worried, what Vallabh would have to say when he saw me all decked up. I thought the *bindi* didn't look too bad on me. And my unusually long neck looked slightly better with the strings of pearls around it. A little bit of beautification – why should it irritate anybody' eyes? As I walked in I saw Vallabh's face anxiously looking into mine. Did I imagine a flash of appreciation in his eyes? On the day of *karva chauth,* seeing your husband's face, after spotting the moon, Basanti had told me, is very auspicious. I felt strangely elated.

Memsaheb tells me I should send Guddi to school. If she goes to school who will look after the baby when I am off to work? Memsaheb doesn't know Guddi goes to wash the utensils in two houses two streets away. When I told her Babloo's Papa wants to take the boys off the school and send them to the carpet factory in Punjab she threw such a tantrum! She said, she would inform the police and we would be punished for making children work. I believe, there is a rule, children below fifteen should not be sent to work. How can I make her understand? For us more children means more hands for work. Am I going to make Babloo and Bittu collectors? She says I am not giving enough food to Guddi. I told her, girls should not be pampered. Who knows what is in store for them? Memsaheb says I have got everything wrong. She tells me my hard-earned money is not to be given away to Babloo's Papa. It is true he blows it up, gambling and drinking. But how can I refuse him? He beats me to pulp. Last time he came home I said I had no money and it was a fact. Whatever I had earned – weaving baskets at the centre where Memsaheb goes – I had handed it over to her and she had put it in the bank. He ransacked the rice tin and toppled the flour sack, the usual places where I hide money and then threatened me if I don't stop working for Memsaheb he would kill me. Someone had been filling his ears. Memsaheb always tells me I should fight back with Babloo's Papa. But the house where a woman raises her voice is doomed. That was what my grandmother and my mother used to say. My mother-in-law had told me the same thing. "They have all been telling you lies," Memsaheb screamed at me.

I don't know how to save Basanti. This time, her husband had come home with a girl. He told the *dhobi*, she was his niece. But everyone knew he was bluffing. Vallabh tells me he had seen him suspiciously sauntering near Jyoti cinema. Someone had told him he was a pimp. When I heard Basanti's loud wailing, I couldn't just control myself. I rushed to their quarters. Her husband was sitting cross-legged on the *charpai* outside the room as though nothing was wrong with anyone at home. The girl who sat by his side stared at me and giggled. The man faced me with a kind of contempt against which I felt awkward and defenceless. "You have come to tempt my wife away? Bring police, bring all those slogan-screaming women from your blessed centre. Let us see who will win?" He looked at me up and down as though he was sizing me up. So bold, so brazen, I was shocked. I saw him getting up and pulling his short frame up with glee as though he knew exactly how to deal with me. It was I who did not know how to deal with him. Slogans and speeches didn't come to my rescue. I stepped back impulsively. Basanti was standing near the window; her face looked red and swollen as though a beehive had broken loose and descended on her.

"Memsaheb, you told me I should protest; I told him, I won't let him take the boys off the school, I won't send them to Punjab, I won't let this slut in. Look, what he has done to me! Get away Memsaheb, leave this house and go. I don't trust this man. He can harm you." I heard her wailing after me.

Malini told me about her harrowing misadventure with Basanti's husband. She shouldn't have worked herself up, especially, now, as she is right into her fifth month. I am quite upset. But I am glad Malini had realised all those enforcement schemes are not so simple as they are made to sound on the podiums. How am I going to tell her our landlord, the bureaucrat, has asked us to vacate the house? She would jump to the conclusion that it has something to do with the morning's mishap. Yes, now that I think of it, it is possible, somebody might have complained...

"Malini, you know my Maasi's flat, the one who has gone to Canada, is lying vacant. Why don't we move into that flat? You will soon need somebody to help you. How can we keep a maid here?" Malini raised her shapely eyebrows. "Okay... Malini, I won't say maid... hmm – we need a domestic help." Malini looked hard at me, obviously not very impressed. It took me almost one week to convince her.

Malini sorted out the clothes and the kitchen stuff and I piled books and files into cartons. As I was separating the trunks and dismantling the settee on the veranda, I heard the shouts and yells outside. Dhobi and his son, Babloo and Bittu were all on the run. With sticks and poles in hands they were chasing someone. Who were they chasing? I called out to them.

"Babuji it is the hen," Dhobi shouted back. "One of the hens has crowed. You know only roosters must crow. It is not natural. It is a bad omen. Something terrible may happen. We must kill this hen." A hen crowing? Nonsense. I knew for sure, it was one of their antics to scare Basanti. *Pakado pakado pakado......* Catch her, catch her ... They were again at it. I could see the poor hen running for her life. Scrambling over the spinach field, she even tried to lift herself up on to the roof, failed and fell on the ground. At last near the fence one of the boys caught her. A frantic flutter, a squeak, a thud – the hen lay limp and lifeless on the flowerbed.

Kokaree ... ko ... The rooster seated theatrically on the tin roof of the poultry shed crowed – a single triumphant call. The red flower on his head gleamed like a crown against the twilight. The hens enclosed in the shed huddled together and clucked ominously in chorus. I pulled the curtains close and shut the green *jafery* door firmly behind. Good, Malini had not come out. It wouldn't have been a good sight for a woman who was expecting her first child.

Anadi's Journey

Bulbul Sharma

In the drowsy heat of the afternoon, the pond lay still and only the shadows of the coconut palms danced on its surface. The air smelt warm and damp as if it was going to rain. Anadi gathered the bundle of wet clothes which his sister had just washed and carried them to a patch of sunlight which fell in a jagged circle near the pond. He lay them out one by one, chasing away the butterfly that swarmed around his head. His mother had told him that if a butterfly ever sat on his right shoulder he would never get married and even at the age of ten Anadi longed to be a householder. He wanted a big house, a pretty wife and tall sons. But the house would not be a thatched one like his village home, which swayed and moaned during the monsoon rains. It would be built with red bricks, held firmly together with cement, have painted walls and a high iron gate and it would not be in Bishtupur but somewhere far away in a shimmering city which Anadi was not certain existed outside his imagination.

Anadi's father had died when he was six months old and his mother, too sick and frail to look after this child of late middle age had given him to her eldest daughter who had no children of her own. Anadi spread the clothes out to dry and then sat down in the shade of the mango tree to read the new book his brother had sent him from Calcutta. Books were not easy to find in this small village of Bishtpur which was a five-hour boat journey from the nearest town. It took two days by boat steamer, train and then finally by bus to reach Calcutta, a city which seemed to Anadi as awesome and unattainable as paradise.

Anadi went every evening to watch the boat arrive at the river bank which was just a few minutes away from his house, behind a grove of banana trees. He sat under a tree, a little away from the crowded jetty, and watched the passengers as they came off the boat, carefully looking for any signs that would tell him something about the city they had just visited. But the men looked as ordinary as they had done when they had left Bishtupur. Their faces did not wear new expressions nor were they surrounded by shining auras which a visit to the city should surely have marked them with. The journey they had undertaken, so full of mystery, danger and excitement, did not seem to have changed them in any way. Anadi often followed them home, listening to their conversation but their voices were the same and they still talked about their debts, about the rice crop and the recent haul of fish as they did when they sat in their courtyards at home. These men had been to Calcutta, the very name made Anadi breathless with joy and fear, They had sat in a train, seen motor cars, heard their blaring horns, and walked down streets lit by gas lights and heard the radio and yet they remained unchanged, still talking like ordinary men of debts, rice and fish.

Anadi felt his ten years a heavy burden which clung to his shoulders, never allowing him to be free. And it was not just him, everyone in the village remained weighed down, standing still in one place, as if afraid to move. The old men sat in a shaded corner of the courtyard, their gnarled hands always holding the stem of the hookah in the same position. The children played the same games over and over near the pond, their bodies thin and agile forever. Their mothers too always wore the same expressions as they quarrelled and laughed amongst themselves. His house, surrounded by evergreen banana and coconut trees, remained unchanged in every season and, day after day, his mother sat in the same dark corner of the kitchen, cleaning an endless quantity of rice.

Anadi knew that another world existed somewhere far away on the other side of the river but he could never reach it because Bishtupur would never let him go. Each day he watched the boat leave Bishtupur without him, feeling as helpless as Kanu the blind boy who could not walk to the pond though he knew it was there.

"Let the boy stay at home now and help you. He is old enough," his mother said, her voice faint with fever, "schools and studies will only make him grow wings and fly away to Calcutta." Anadi sat near her bed, hoping that if he did not make a noise they would forget about taking him away from school. "No, Ma, he is a very bright boy and studies hard. Not like the other boys in the school. This one will go far, maybe even to an English college in Calcutta. Let him finish his matriculation and try for a scholarship," his brother-in-law said. Anadi suddenly felt free, as if all his fears had floated away out of the window above his mother's bed and, no longer afraid to be seen, he ran out of the house. It seemed to him that the entire village had changed and the people, the houses, the trees all swirled around him and even the pond was no longer stagnant and still, but rippled with new shades of green.

The boat tossed about on the edge of the bank, its ropes straining as the passengers pushed their way forward to find a place. As the boat moved away, Bishtupur became smaller and smaller and then finally disappeared. Anadi felt it had merged into the world waiting for him across the river and he knew he was not leaving but only forming a bridge between his childhood and adult life.

The dolphins jumped out of the water, forming an arc over the waves and then disappeared into the sea. Anadi waited for them to appear but they seem to have vanished deep into some secret hiding place beneath the ocean. The ship moved in a wavy, uneven line cutting through the grey blue waters like a blunt knife. Anadi wondered if the river in Bishtupur had also merged into this vast ocean and leaned over the railing as if he could see traces of the muddy river in the ocean and then he laughed at his own foolishness.

"Not seasick any more, boy?" asked an elderly Bengali gentleman as he strolled past. He wore a white suit with a big hat and carried a cane which he kept tapping on the deck like a blind man. "I tell everyone it is the boiled cabbage on the ship that makes people sick, not the sea. Though we have been away from Calcutta only for a week I already miss my mother's cooking. Mustard fish and banana flower curry … coconut prawns ... Oh Ma ...," he sighed as he looked far into the ocean as if waiting for his mother to suddenly emerge out of the sea. Anadi was surprised that such an old man still had a mother who was alive. She must be ninety at least. My mother is a hundred and one years old and still supervises the cooking at home. My wife is terrified of her," said the old man suddenly breaking into English. "Must practice your English, young man. Practice makes your English perfect. Every morning, while brushing your teeth, recite to yourself all the difficult verbs, especially the present continuous tense which we Bengalis find so difficult," he said and began to mutter, "have been eating, have been bathing, have been sick..." Then he walked away tapping his cane.

Anadi wished he had stayed back to talk to him. He seemed like a well travelled man and would know everything about England. It was lonely on this huge ship which was as big as all Bishtupur and had more people in it. Anadi could not stop comparing his village to every new thing he saw. Calcutta, frightening with its endless streams of people and black clouds of smoke had seemed to him like a monster raging in a storm. This was not the city of his dreams. But he had spent three happy years in the Scottish Church College where he had got a scholarship to study after his matriculation from the village school. He remembered how the entire village had come to the river bank to see him off and his mother too had come out of the house for the first time in his life. She seemed much younger in the daylight, almost like a stranger. "Bathe every day and do not eat beef," she had whispered to him and then left without looking back. Her face appeared before him now and he felt like crying out "Ma..." like the old man had done. He knew he would see her again when he returned home because she would never leave her dark corner in the kitchen.

The dishes swayed gently on the table and Anadi hesitated though everyone else had already begun to eat. "Is it beef?" he whispered to the old gentleman who was sitting next to him. "No, it is veal, delicious, but put some pepper on it first." Relieved because the aroma from the steaming dish was making his mouth water, Anadi quickly began to eat.

"I had to throw my sacred thread into the river after that. How could I explain to my mother that veal was not related to seal?" he said as the laughter died down. His German was quite fluent now, in fact much better than his English which held traces of his village accent. In London, the other Indians had often made fun of his English and he remembered his first day at the Royal College of Mines. "Just arrived from the paddy fields?" A tall young man asked him in Bengali, mimicking his village dialect. "Yes, do you know my village – Bishtupur?" Anadi asked eagerly. "No, my friend, I don't. But I can smell the mustard oil and recognise those Kahnai tailor clothes from far," he replied in English as the group of boys cackled with laughter. England was freezing cold with grey skies and greyer buildings. It never stopped raining. This was not his village rain which raged through in a brief flash of temper, washing the trees clean and making the coconuts and mangoes drop into their courtyard. It was not the frightening monsoon which created havoc but then receded to leave the land fertile and green. The rain here was like the continuous weeping of an old woman to whose sorrow everyone had become indifferent. People did not stay indoors when it rained, watching it fearfully from their windows as he had done, they put on their raincoats, opened their umbrellas and walked about as if it was normal weather.

Anadi was happy to leave England and sad too because he had made friends with a few English boys. But the last four months had erased the picture of a glorious, golden land which he had read about and admired all through school and college. This was not the England of his dreams and these timid, grey men, always clutching umbrellas, were not the mighty rulers of his country but imposters who had somehow taken over England.

Calcutta, London... both the cities had let him down like old, trusted friends who had turned into enemies. But Frieburg, a small town in Germany that he never knew and which had no expectations to live up to, was perfect. Anadi liked the unhurried, friendly pace of the town and its crowd of young students. Old men sat in sunlit parks and children played familiar games on the empty streets. In 1931 Germany was brimming with over confidence and it infected the youth and filled them with a sense of their own importance.

"Anadi, you must eat well or you will become thin and what will your mother say?" said Mutti as she placed a huge plate of meat and potatoes in front of him. Knowing well that his mother would rather he starve than eat beef, Anadi quickly began to eat before the muttering of his mother's voice in his head became too loud. Mutti, his landlady, had adopted him from the first day he appeared on her doorstep, lean and hungry, unable to speak a word of German. He looked at her kind face and wondered if she had been his mother in another life.

When he received his Doctorate in Engineering, she was the one who celebrated with a huge cake and tears of joy while his own relatives in Calcutta were somewhat bewildered. "You went to become an engineer but now you say you are a doctor?" The day he left Germany, Anadi heard Hitler's voice on the radio and as the words raged in anger, he suddenly knew that the world he was leaving would never be the same again.

"The girl is very pretty but she has lived in Delhi most of her life. Hope she is not too smart," his uncle said. Anadi nodded vaguely, too nervous to speak. "The girl's father is a Government officer, plays tennis with the British but luckily her mother is very orthodox. So shake hands with the father and touch the mother's feet."

Anadi, overcome by stage fright, did exactly the opposite much to everyone's amazement. "He has just come from Germany," said his uncle and the relatives, assembled to inspect him, seemed satisfied with this explanation. Since the father was 'modern', he was allowed to see the girl. But her face was a hazy blur and all that he could remember was she was very short and had thick wavy hair. "Wasn't she slightly plump?" he asked his aunt, hoping she would describe her. "It is good to be plump. Some clever mothers make their daughters wear two or three petticoats to make them look nice and plump," said his aunt, who was pleased with the match.

After fifty years and four children, Meera was as plump as ever with a thick mane of gleaming black hair. Anadi was terrified of his wife whose diminutive size packed a fiery temper which flared up at the oddest of things but remained calm in the face of danger. Though just nineteen, she had travelled with him to the lonely towns in remote areas where his work as an engineer took him. In Giridi they had lived in a huge, dilapidated bungalow which was haunted and Meera read *The Canterville Ghost* aloud every evening hoping to lure the resident ghost. In Bhilai she had turned a snake filled pit into a lovely garden and when he landed the car on the verandah during his first and last attempt at driving, she had just laughed. In Burnpore she taught herself the correct English etiquette to deal with the haughty British ladies. Mutti had taught him how to eat with a fork and knife but he still got confused sometimes and had once tried to cut through a layer of spaghetti as it streamed down his chin. The entire restaurant had applauded him when he finally succeeded with one final slash and cut off the spaghetti like an expert barber chopping off a full grown beard.

Meera and he had lived in so many different homes; in so many cities yet he remembered the name and number on each gate, the colour of the curtains, the trees in the garden, the names of their neighbours and the dogs they had had. "This is a Burnpore story." "No – a Bhilai one, it has Honey and Sarala in it ..." his children would argue when he travelled back to retrace his life. His children, of whom he was so proud, were very different from him and he wondered what they would say if ever he took them back to Bishtupur. Would his son, a brilliant student at the medical college, sit under the mango tree and read all through the day as he had done? His daughters, so smart and knowledgeable about everything in the world, who had already travelled to various parts of the world at an age when he had never set eyes on a bicycle, would they walk to the pond to collect mangoes after a storm?

Bishtupur was so far now, much further than the outside world had been when he stood by the river, waiting. It was in another country now and his village existed only in his memory and yet it was closer and more real than ever before.

Anadi put his book down on the table and looked out of the window. A strange sound, which he had heard half a century ago, suddenly floated up to him. He opened the door and went out. An old man stood at the gate carrying a basket full of small paper packets. "Sahib, you want coconut sweets?" he asked in broken Hindi. "Are you from Khulna district?" Anadi asked, his tongue savouring the dialect after so many years. "Yes ... yes ... Dada ...," the man replied, happy to speak in his own language in this strange city. They both began talking at once. Coconut palms swayed above him and the pond rippled in the sun. Anadi could smell the wet earth by the river and he heard the village women call out to their children in shrill voices.

When the youngest daughter came home from college, she found her father sitting on the floor of the drawing room with a strange, bedraggled man in a white dhoti. Sounds of laughter filled the house and their voices spoke in a strange language which sounded familiar but she could not understand a word. Her father's voice had lost its firm deep tone and he now talked in an excited, high pitched, almost childish voice.

Anadi saw his daughter watching him from the door but did not call her in. What could she have to say to this old man from a village near Khulna? He was as alien to her as she was to him and only Anadi could link them together. This stranger who sold coconut sweets and jaggery from door to door understood him more than his beloved daughter.

"Tell me did you have a deaf teacher in your school called Kanai?"

"Yes, and a headmaster who gave us a holiday every second day because he wanted to sleep."

"Do you remember the fish that swam into the paddy fields after the rains and the way the coconuts fell on our heads during a storm?"

Together, they created their village once more. It was as if he had left his beloved family, this house built with bricks and cement in a city he admired, and slowly erasing the decades of journeys, years of adapting to the unfamiliar, he had now gone home to Bishtupur.

In Memory of Meera

Madhu Tandan

The strangest events happened after Shanta attended a prayer meeting held in remembrance of a dead woman. A woman she had only vaguely heard about, but never met. Shanta's father had rung her to say that Meera, a distant relative, had died three days ago. Since Meera had lived all her life in the hills and few knew her in Delhi, could she come and attend the prayer meeting?

When Shanta arrived there were ten or twelve people sitting quietly facing a garlanded photograph, in front of which incense sticks burnt steadily. The picture was that of a woman in her mid-forties; my own age Shanta had thought with surprise. Her eyes were gentle, tinged with a thoughtful sadness, as though she had seen suffering and had tried to understand it. Despite that, the woman in the photograph smiled with genuine warmth that drew

Shanta to her. She is a person I would have liked to know, Shanta admitted to herself, and was startled by her own thought.

After a few minutes one of the men rose and said, "Meera *didi* was a very upright woman, a true pillar of strength to her family and friends. Her goodness of heart and generosity of spirit will be remembered by each of us. She may have broken the prison of this body and left, but she will remain in our hearts guiding us with her strength and wisdom."

These were standard words spoken at prayer meetings for the dead, but they said nothing of who this woman was, and perhaps no one really knew. There is something about a prayer meeting that reminds you that, one day, your own garlanded photograph may be resting on a similar table and other people will gather together to condole your death. And what will they say about my life, Shanta mused? Probably, that I was an ordinary receptionist, in a Government hospital, and that my life was far removed from the world spinning around me. A world of computers, travel and change. Yet no change intrudes my world, where every day I sit behind a desk whose hinges are broken, and make one folder after another for the endless line of patients waiting to be seen. A hospital where the doctors are overworked, the medicines are in short supply, and the sanction for new equipment never comes.

The hospital Shanta worked for was on indefinite strike, so she went home after the prayer meeting. An odd restlessness overtook her as she confronted the lonely silence of her home. Her work at the hospital left her so tired, that besides cooking herself a simple meal at night, she had energy to do little else. She was a shy person who had few friends, and no hobby to fall back on. She considered switching on the television, but all the serials she enjoyed watching came after eight o'clock in the evening. What was she to do with herself now?

Then, something odd happened. She suddenly felt she was not alone in the room. Startled she looked around, but found no one. I'm just lonely, she thought, but could not dispel the feeling that a moment ago someone had been standing right behind her. Shanta shock her head to banish the thought and went to the tiny kitchen to make a cup of tea.

While she sipped her tea she looked up, and there, for just a moment, was Meera's face imprinted on the opposite wall. Shanta blinked, looked again, but it was gone. I'm imagining it! I don't even know who this woman was. Why should I see her face? But Meera seemed to have been asking her a question, and Shanta had the oddest feeling that the silence in the room was waiting for her answer.

Shanta's life did not afford her the luxury of flights of imagination; what she could not see, touch, taste or hear did not really exist for her. Yet why was she left with the sense that there was someone in the room, even though her eyes could not see who it was? A humming sensation began in her head. It filled her ears and shut the world outside. Without her conscious volition she took a pen and began to write. Barring the occasional letter to her mother, Shanta had never written anything before, but now she was writing as though she was long familiar with the art. Her pen moved fast across the page as she wrote:

Since the age of ten my eyes perceived the world differently than other people. Life seemed like a web of forces, whose intersecting points I could see. Below the known, I often glimpsed the unknown.

My mother once said to me, "Uncle Rajendra is coming to see us at tea-time."

Instinctively I replied, "Oh! But he won't be able to come. He'll be called away."

Uncle Rajendra did ring, shortly before he was due to arrive, apologising to my mother that he would not be able to have tea with her as he had been unexpectedly detained.

After such episodes had been repeated a few times, my mother would entreat me, "Don't say such things because when you do, they seem to come true."

I wondered what made me say the things I did? Soon I recognised that I saw behind the swirl of everyday events another reality, which knew the real outcome of an event. And I, for a while, became its wise and innocent voice. People often thought along a particular line, but the event was moving in just the opposite direction. And I had to hold the knowledge of both worlds simultaneously.

When I met people, sometimes, I saw images flash past me, as though I was being shown snapshots of their lives. They seemed to hover over their heads, like when my cousin Arati, was enthusiastically recounting how she had been accepted for her first job, I saw a very different image surround her.

Instead, of an office, I saw her dressed in bridal clothes. I don't know what everyone must have thought when I interrupted the conversation by saying, "You are going to get married soon." Arati stopped mid-sentence, looked at my mother as though I was crazy and said, "Meera, you have not even been listening to what I have been saying."

Before Arati could join work, her parents introduced her to a boy settled in America. Three weeks later they were married, and Arati had flown with her husband to America.

This power found expression in my life in another form when Moti, my cocker spaniel, my one companion in my solitary ways, fell ill. When I was a child, Moti would put his head on my lap as I read, would walk with me in the green sanctuary of trees behind our house, and sleep at the foot of my bed every night. He was all I needed for company. But one day he began to vomit and soon he could not retain any food. My parents and I rushed him to the doctor, but none of the medicines had any effect. He just lay in a corner with his eyes closed, neither eating nor drinking.

My father said gently to me, "I think he is dying, Meera."

I wept and kept saying, "He cannot Papa, he is my best friend."

My father held and rocked me in his arms.

That evening I put Moti on my lap and gently ran my hands over his golden fur again and again. I had no idea how long I sat there; all I know is that my hands had became hot and sweaty, and his fur damp before I fell asleep. On the second night, as I sat stroking Moti, he opened his eyes and tried to sit up. By the third night he sipped a little water, and after that he slowly began to recover. My mother told everyone, "It was Meera's love that brought Moti back to life. It was a miracle."

I never knew what it really was. The only memory I had of those dark nights was my hands turning soft and limpid, following some invisible rhythm. Maybe that was the first time I felt that the wounds of pain can draw out the hands that heal.

My mother felt it too. Whenever she had a headache, she would ask me to place my hands on her forehead. Then I would press her temples and move to the centre of the forehead and feel her flesh first crease then ease under my fingertips. Slowly, she would relax and murmur, "You have magic in your hands, beta."

The phone rang four times before Shanta heard it. The pen dropped from her hand, she felt she had been jerked out of sleep. She stared at the page and slowly began to read the words. It was her handwriting all right, but nothing else belonged to her. Neither the story, nor the words. It was too far removed from anything in her life. The phone continued to ring. She walked towards it, in a daze, unsure what was happening to her.

It was her father: "Beta, your aunt Anju wants me to go to Maniagar, the small village in the hills where Meera had lived. She needs someone to sort out her papers and clear her belongings."

Shanta felt surrounded by Meera. She did not respond to her father's words.

"Hello, Shanta, can you hear me?"

Finally she replied, "Yes, Papa. How come none of us ever met Meera?"

"She was a recluse who never came down to the plains."

"What did she do there?"

"She was some kind of doctor or healer. Her mother always said that Meera had magic in her hands. She had the power to heal."

Shanta put down the phone and groped for a chair to sit down, feeling loose-limbed with shock. A healer... Meera was a healer, and the words that had poured out of her, a few minutes ago, was the story of just such a woman. What is going on! What kind of a bizarre coincidence is this? I'm writing the story of a dead woman I never knew. Shanta shook her head in disbelief. This cannot be happening to me.

Shanta got up slowly and looked out of the window where she saw other sooty multi-storeyed buildings, point their dirty fingers to the sky. The walls of her home, and hospital were the limits of her world. They protected her from the unknown. When she looked into the mirror, she saw tired eyes that expected nothing from life but the safety of habit. No all-consuming love had ever crossed her path, nor searing hate had ever ripped her asunder. She lived in a twilight zone where the depth and height of her emotions were confined to the simple and acceptable. To discuss a recipe with a colleague, to talk about the water shortage in her flat, or predict the outcome of the next episode in her favourite serial were the definitions of her reality. But suddenly something strange had walked into her life, and she was afraid. Maybe I need to get out of the house and not think of this again, Shanta thought. She quickly went to the table, collected all the pages she had written, and tore them into tiny bits, throwing them into the dustbin. She then left the house.

That night she had a vivid dream:

Meera was sitting at a large desk, worn old with use. Scattered over it were books and papers. She looks up from her writings and says, "Won't you help finish my story? I couldn't finish it because I had to leave suddenly."

Early in the morning, with her eyes still closed, Shanta's mind swam for a few seconds between dream and reality. Where was she? Slowly the bedroom came into focus with the familiar calendar of Ganesh on the opposite wall. This was her own room but why did she feel she had actually spoken to Meera in some other house... a house with a study and an age-worn desk and chair, which had a dull maroon cushion on it.

'Won't you help me finish my story? I couldn't finish it...' Meera's words hung in the room when Shanta questioned aloud, "How can I? Why should I? ...." Then she remembered that, in the dream, Meera had gently requested, and not ordered her. The dream was so real that Shanta felt she had finally met Meera for the first time.

The clock by Shanta's bedside ticked away, measuring the minutes of her indecision. Finally she rose from her bed and rang up Aunt Anju, the only person who may know something more about Meera. "I hear you are going to sort out Meera's papers in Maniagar," Shanta said.

"Thank God! Your father is coming to help me."

"Aunt, did Meera ever write anything? I mean was she some kind of writer?"

"I believe so. She had published a book on medicinal herbs found in the Himalayan foothills. I have not read it. She was such a private person. All her life she lived in that tiny cottage, tending to the sick villagers of that area. Her mother said that she would retire to her study in the evenings and write."

"Had she started writing down anything about her life, I mean about her own life story?"

"Not that I know of."

There was a pause in the conversation; Shanta prolonged the silence giving herself time to make up her mind. She held her breath and then slowly let it out. She then asked quietly, "May I come with you and Papa to Maniagar?"

"Of course, my dear. I'll welcome an extra pair of hands. It's always so difficult, and sad, to clear up the house of someone who has gone."

They reached Maniagar, on a May afternoon. The wheat was ripening on the terraced hills, and the mountain air smelt of pine and resin. It was a small cottage, with a sloping slate roof and wooden beams that were dark with age, tucked away behind a clump of pine trees. Ganga Singh, the old retainer of the house, who had served Meera for twenty years, came out to greet them.

Quietude descended on Shanta as she stepped into the cottage. The owner had left her presence like a prayer in the rooms. It was not just the sheer simplicity of the cottage with its three chairs in the lobby, a small bedroom where a rolled up mattress, a chest of drawers, and a bookshelf were considered the only necessities, that struck her. It was more the feeling that the person who had lived in this house knew that her sojourn in this life was that of a traveller who was passing through, and who could not afford the indulgence of creating the illusion of permanence. Meera had lived in this cottage for twenty years, but probably had left it without a backward glance. Except maybe for one room whose door was closed.

Shanta asked Ganga Singh, "Is this another bedroom?"

"No, that is *Didi's* study. She used to work there. I've not touched anything because she liked her papers to remain as she left them."

Shanta felt a reluctance to enter the study, as though that would signal her commitment to a dead woman's request. But Ganga Singh had already opened the door and was beckoning her to enter. In the centre of the book-lined study was a large age-worn desk and chair identical to her dream. The chair had the same dull maroon cushion on it! Shanta felt if she looked at the desk from the corner of her eye, she might see Meera sitting on the chair, and quietly asking her, 'Won't you help finish my story?'

And this time Shanta knew she had to give an answer.

She moved towards the desk with a familiarity born from her dream. All kinds of papers lay on the desk – notes on patients she had treated, recipes of herbs, account papers, and books. Instinctively she started rummaging through the papers, searching for something; something she was not even sure existed. Then she saw a faded blue folder in which she found some typewritten sheets. It began:

Since the age of ten my eyes perceived the world differently than other people. Life seemed like a web of forces, whose intersecting points I could see. Below the known, I often glimpsed the unknown.

My mother once said to me, "Uncle Rajendra is coming to see us at tea-time."

Instinctively I replied, "Oh! But he won't be able to come.

He'll be called away."

Uncle Rajendra did ring...

Every incident from Uncle Rajendra coming to tea, to Arati's wedding, to Moti's illness and her mother's headaches had already been written by Meera before she had died. How was I sitting three hundred miles away, writing the same story, without knowing anything about Meera? Shanta held her head in her hands totally stunned. This was a dead woman's unfinished manuscript about her life.... What is happening to me, Shanta thought? What am I doing here? Why is Meera asking me to finish her manuscript for her? I am no writer. But I didn't write the story; it seemed to have been dictated to me. And, what is the rest of her story?

Shanta decided to go for a very long walk. When she returned she went straight to Meera's study, sat down and began writing:

In these hills, I have seen the face of courage. If the rains come late, the crop dies, and the villagers go hungry. If the rain comes too soon, the wheat rots and again they have little to eat. Yet there is no searing sense of injustice in their hearts as they battle with their poverty, the poor soil, their lack of education and health care. They seem to know that there will be no real changes in their lives, and that their small and fragmented land holdings will never be enough to feed them. Yet they are capable of such generosity of spirit as they unexpectedly turn up at my doorstep with a little curd, milk, or ghee as a gift.

There is so much I want to do for them. But for the time being the back of my house has become their dispensary where some medicines, antiseptic, cotton and gauze helps me dress a sickle wound, or attend to a persistent cough, or treat a sprained wrist. And there are other times when I just sit with my hands on the ailing part of a child, letting that mysterious life force quicken within my hands. Where does this power come from which clears my mind, so that not a single thought defiles it, as it flows silently to bridge the distance between that crying, sick child in my lap and the hands that heal? I do not know who does it or how it happens. All I know is that the hand I place on the child soothes it, so that its persistent crying quietens down to find relief in sleep.

First only the men came. Then they brought their women and children, till one day I was surprised to see one of them carrying a sick goat in his arms to be cured. Then followed a blur of humans and animals sitting on my back veranda waiting their turn.

When I lay my hands on the problem area something strange begins to happen. I feel the sensation of pinpricks on the tips of my fingers as heat pours into my hands. I know then that it has begun. When my hands begin to cool and stiffen I know I can do no more. I withdraw my hands and then wait for the tide to come in again. A power greater than the body, wider than the mind, deeper than heart heals the sick, and I, for a while, become its privileged witness.

Shanta stopped writing and looked out of the window. The evening hour was galloping towards darkness, the trees silently accepting the verdict. She looked at the pen lying across the paper and realised that she liked the woman she was writing about. No falsity marred the gift Meera had. She seemed to act like a caretaker of a power, which she dispensed willingly, without making any claims of ownership.

There was a knock on the door. Ganga Singh entered with a cup of tea. She asked him, "How had *Didi* died?"

"She died in her sleep. The entire village collected outside the house when they heard the news."

"Probably, they loved her very much."

"She helped so many of us. We believe that God had given her a gift. Whenever we laid a sick child in her lap, we were sure the child would recover. She helped all of us till she was exhausted. But she knew other things also.

"Once a villager said to her, 'I hope the rains come on time.'

"She said gently to him, 'Ramu, they could be delayed this year.'

"And sure enough they were." Ganga Singh said with respect in his voice.

"If we went to sell our potatoes she would say, 'You'll get a good price this year.' Whenever she said that, we would."

"She died young," Shanta remarked.

"But she knew about her death," Ganga Singh replied promptly.

"What do you mean?"

"Fifteen days before her death she stood outside this house, watching the sunrise, when I brought her a cup of tea. She turned to me and said, 'Gangada I won't be here for long. My time has come. It has been a good life, and I have no regrets.' Then she shook her head as though to deny her own words. 'No I have one regret. A deep regret. I could not pass on what I know to someone else. Who will look after my people when I am gone?'"

Ganga Singh's eyes filled with tears, "I remember her so often. But she warned me that she was going. Only I wouldn't believe her."

His words echoed in the air, long after he had left. Meera knew of her death and the only regret she had was not for herself. Who was this woman called Meera? No sooner had the thought crossed Shanta's mind that she felt a strong bond with this woman she never knew. She seemed like an old friend she had lost contact with, but had now rediscovered. Her life and mine are as different as chalk and cheese. Yet, I am sitting on her desk as though by the strength of a long association. She fills this room with her presence, and now by a strange twist of events my life too.

Next morning Ganga Singh came to Shanta and said, "A man from the adjoining village has come. He had not heard about *Didi's* death, till I told him. Your father and aunt are asleep. Would you like to meet him?"

Shanta walked through the house to the back courtyard. There stood a villager with a crying child in his arms. The villager said sadly, "I didn't know *Didi* had died. I cannot believe it. I have walked two hours to get here, only to learn she is no more. Six months ago *Didi* helped me when a nail got embedded in my heel. She pulled it out and dressed it. Now where do I go with this child?"

"What is wrong with your child?"

"She does not eat anything and cries all the time. She has become so thin that she is wasting away."

"You must show her to a doctor."

"Which doctor? Where? They are miles from here."

"I wish I could help you, but I do not know what is wrong with your child," Shanta had to raise her voice above the shrill cries of the child.

Her father rocked the child while Ganga Singh went to get some water, to moisten the child's lips. She only bunched her small fists and cried louder. Huge tears drenched her eyes as she tried to express her discomfort in the only way she could.

"Where is the child's mother?"

"She is tending the cattle. Only one of us could come."

Shanta turned to Ganga Singh and asked, "How far is the nearest doctor?"

"About fifteen miles away."

"Can we take the child there?"

"Yes, we can, but it will not be open at this early hour."

"We'll wait for a while. In the meantime, Gangada, could you make this man a cup of tea? He has come a long way."

When the tea arrived, Shanta went forward to relieve the

villager of his crying child. She put the child in her lap and rocked her for a few moments. She placed her left hand on the child's brow and soothed it. Her other hand she rested on the child's hollow stomach. Shanta felt heat rushing to her palms as they travelled to her fingertips, in a mysterious dance. The bleating of the goats, the rustle of trees in conference, the gentle hum of the wind all seemed to stop for a moment in expectation. Nature seemed to pause. Shanta, however, heard none of these. Her whole body seemed motionless, lost in some deep reverie. Only her hands moved gently over the child's stomach. When Shanta came around she realised that the child had stopped crying.

She looked up to see Ganga Singh and the villager staring at her as though they had witnessed a miracle.

It was then that Shanta knew that she would not be leaving the hills of Maniagar, ever.

Bhadoo

Uma Vasudev

Mrs Dixit's husband had already signed the rent lease for a year for their new house when she learnt that their landlord was going to be the notorious Bhadoo, the lecherous old grain merchant who was known to have an eye for women in general and little girls in particular. Mrs Dixit was horrified. Her own daughter was just eleven. Niloo. Born after years of repeated disappointments. At 50, Mrs Dixit felt almost shy at being her mother, but she was fiercely solicitous nevertheless, perhaps because of it. So everything regarding Niloo had to be perfect, and perfect, to the determined meticulousness of Mrs Dixit's character meant just right. The right food, the right clothes, the right friends, also the right feelings. For, felt Mrs Dixit, there must be a decorum not only about behaviour but even about one's inner motivations. She saw to it therefore that Niloo was properly impregnated by the values that she herself cherished above all, decency, courtesy and truthfulness. Naturally too, Mrs Dixit was particularly careful that Niloo should not be impelled to draw upon an awareness that she was a rich man's daughter.

It had been a blow to Mrs Dixit to discover that she couldn't expect the same teaching for Niloo from her school. Her teacher, a pretentiously adolescent creature, had once scoffed at Niloo's complaint that she feared her pen had been stolen by exclaiming: "So what? You're a rich girll Why don't you ask your parents to buy you another?" She had even made it a point to single out Niloo again and again to taunt her about her advantages when the rest of her schoolmates had to make do with ragged comforts. That was the worst, thought Mrs Dixit of small town minds. But with her usual determination she decided that Niloo must be made to feel as normal and ordinary as any other little girl of her age. It was to the greater credit of Mrs Dixit than to the natural innocence of a child that Niloo, despite having everything, never turned into one of those obnoxious brats that spring from over-indulgent parents.

Nor indeed did she develop, and that of course she owed to the fortune of her circumstances, that pathetic maturity which comes with the early assumption of responsibility which marked her poorer counterparts, especially in a small town such as they lived in. Like them, she might have had to be helping her mother with the cooking, or looking after a baby brother or do the marketing and become so imbued though unconsciously with the gestures of womanhood that it was never difficult to associate them with its fundamentals. Little women they were, with their saris draped round their in-grown contours and their soft hair drawn tightly into a bun and their faces looking pinched with a forced courage. It was quite tragic, and Mrs Dixit, at times, could not bear to see or even feel it. You could visualise them being seduced she would realise and not be shocked. That was what was so horrible, Perhaps that is how Bhadoo... But Niloo, Niloo remained the child that she was, with soft grey eyes, deep brown hair braided into two plaits and a shy, tender, smile. It was unthinkable that Niloo … that Bhadoo ... that it could be at all. It was unthinkable anyway for Mrs Dixit was a deeply. deeply moral person with a persistent faith in human nature. Her sense of discipline was itself controlled by a warm sympathy and if she was offended by an act of impropriety she was equally hurt by the motivations of evil.

But for the first time Rami Dixit did feel afraid. And for the first time she felt she couldn't tackle the situation with that calm, practical sense and resilient will that marked all her other actions. How was she going to cope with a year, a year of what would have to be unbearable surveillance? Strangely enough, when her husband came home from work in the evening and she saw his pale, nervous face as he said, "I couldn't work at all. I'll never forgive myself if anything happens to Niloo," she found herself hardening instead of being able to offer him that tearful sympathy that he possibly expected of her. A show of weakness always did that to her. It acted like a challenge to her immense reserves of fortitude. She squared her shoulders mentally. It was a man they had to deal with, after all, she thought, not a beast. Whatever it was that had raised him to the level of the human must and could be turned towards rational behaviour. She did not quite realise how vast was the significance of her faith, nor indeed, how much of it she was going to put at atake …

"We'll not allow him to enter our flat, even if he is our landlord," Kundan was saving, "I shall write to him if there's anything to be said about the house. You must warn Niloo that he's no *manu* or *chahcha* and if ever I learn that she has accepted sweets or chocolates from him or even waited to hear him say anything, I shall thrash her blue."

"Kundan!"

"You don't seem to understand what we're up against, Rami. I wouldn't stay here a minute if I could help it."

"But he can't be so bad. Why do they let him live amongst them? If he were so dangerous … "

"He's rich," said Kundan simply. "What's more, its the regard they had for his father. A jewel of a man, I'm told. Its his memory they keep inviolate by being tolerant of the son. You know the fetish we make of loyalty …"

"But …"

She knew, for instance, that Dadu Narendra Singh, the head of the oldest and most respected families of the area, wore diamonds in his ears, but it seemed to enhance the manhood of his strong, burly figure as she had seen him many a time standing in the corner of a room at a party, his embroidered shawl thrown across his chest and over the shoulder, and in summer, in his white, muslin *kurta*, elegant *dhoti* and the tight *juties* turning upwards at the toes, embroidered in silver and gold. Some of the younger ones would stroll down the main street of the little town on summer evenings with a garland of *motia* flowers wound lightly round their wrists which they would raise to their faces from time to time and smell with exquisite shivers of delight. The *motia* flower had a unique, nostalgic fragrance which wafted through one's blood the recurrent nuances of India's past, sensitive as the smell of a woman's skin, and as evocative of timeless associations. Oh yes. Rami Dixit had a 'thing' about the *motia* flower. But when it came to seeing poor Bhadoo no, no, the wretched Bhadoo, clutching the delicately woven string of flowers in his hand, she made herself see in it the smell of decadence; of the flower that cloyed over sweet in the greedy hands of pimps at prostitute corners, so that Bhadoo could not, must not, must never seem to her to be the affluent simpleton that his obvious status and manner suggested but as one of those shrill-eyed, eagle-mouthed males with mascaraed lashes and pungently perfumed clothes who stood as the heralds of lust in the dark: lean, nightmarish creatures, she remembered as she was driven through that area one night, whose long, yes, long and supple fingers clawed at the closed windows of the car in a preliminary attack of seduction as it crawled past in determined opposition. But Bhadoo was fat. A fat pimp. The mere idea would generate a faint rumble in her stomach which would turn into a grunt and a roar and ultimately into boisterous laughter. Make her blind to danger. To Bhadoo. To Niloo's threatened childhood. Did she lack that moral compass she thought in panic, which could point the direction in critical times to right, wrong, good and evil, to the north, west, south and east of value ....? To have to decide for yourself each time how irredeemable a human being was can be shattering. Yes, shattering decided Rami Dixit. Not that it was wholly a matter of knowing. Knowing made one cruel. Instinct was her compass. Bountiful, tolerant, invariably connecting only with shades of goodness. She sighed. It always landed her into trouble.

It made her lonely too, for her argument then had to interact only with itself, and not with the more arguable, established precepts and their cut and dried protagonists. Like her husband, for instance, who could say that "good is good and bad is bad." It was the easiest way out. So that then she could spit at Bhadoo as if he were a pariah dog and not a human being.

He was certainly fat, thought Rami Dixit, as she saw Bhadoo for the first time that morning. But there was no lascivious glint in his eye as he spoke softly and obsequiously: "Is the *Bai* comfortable in her new house? The roof didn't leak In the rain last night, did it? I thought I should find out ..."

"That's kind of you, thank you, Everything is all right. My ... my husband will talk to you if there's anything that ... er ... we ..."

"I hope we meet often, being such close neighbours now. Is Mr Dixit home? What time does he return from the courts?"

Niloo was plucking at her sari.

"Niloo, love, run along ... There's nothing to be done about the house, thank you, Bhadooji," said Rami, adding the respectful 'ji' with dignity, "It was nice of you to enquire ..." and she began to close the door gradually, inch by inch.

"'I'll call again when Dixitji is home, eh? We should be like brothers now!"

"Yes, of course, yes." She bolted the door and then fell tremulously against it. He must have seen Niloo, she thought. But his attention hadn't wavered for a second from what he had been saying. And then, oh, she thought, I can't believe it. He didn't seem so bad. Perhaps it wasn't true what they said about his fascination for little girls. You could think of evil in the abstract. But you couldn't see a man, talk to him of normal things and brand him irrevocably evil. At least she couldn't. Specially if it were a fat man, she argued and found that insidious laughter beginning to ruffle her body. How was it possible to associate Bhadoo's flabby features and rotund belly, a sort of a benign, good-humoured belly, it seemed, with such a deliberate vice? Perhaps he didn't exploit his weakness with a knowing zest. Perhaps he was subject to an impulsive lust which he couldn't control like a seed within him that burst not into flower but into pus and smell and black blood in which case, he was ill, not evil. No, no, no, he was bad. He must be wholly bad. She must think of him as bad, evil. She had to be careful, wary, tense. She had to make herself afraid. Afraid of this fat, sloppy man with his nervous mouth and his childish desires to please.

So when she happened to meet Bhadoo on the stairs, on the street or in a shop, and she saw his well oiled hair turned to a curl on one side of his forehead, she told herself it was grotesque, not amusing. She knew that many men belonging to landowning families indulged in idiosyncrasies of fashion bequeathed by an age and time which didn't pit manliness against a desire to decorate themselves.

"The bastard. He pretends he's insane whenever any charge is proferred against him, and to prove it, he actually rushes off to the asylum in Nagpur and lives there for two or three months till everything blows over!"

Mrs Dixit's fears dissolved and a lightness blew through her comfortable body like a mass of feathers teasing each point they touched into an irrepressible giggle, into ripples of hysterical amusement. What an infectious bit of roguery that, the thought, trying hard to keep a straight face, as her body heaved and turned and gushed with silent laughter. At the same time she felt another fear taking root. the fear of not being afraid.

"Oh, but imagine going off willingly to an asylum!" she couldn't help exclaiming. "Like one goes for rest to a hill station!"

Kundan looked aghast at her levity. "Have you gone crazy?"

The next morning she found Bhadoo at her doorstep, peering in through the half open door. Fat, grotesque, lascivious, as her husband had said. But with a timid manner and eyes blood red from a constant intake of *bhang*, he had added sternly as if to rebuke her for her "unfortunate lack of proper appreciation of the situation." He wondered how any aspect of this matter could induce in her even the tiniest fraction of a smile. Rami Dixit sighed. Kundan was indeed a very intense person. Not that there was anything in Mrs Dixit either that was frivolous. In fact, that way they were an ideally suited couple, and beneath the regard they had developed for each other over the years, there was sometimes a gesture, sometimes a look which indicated a more tender base, so that you could say, if it could be applied to so staid, proper and dignified a couple, that they were in love with each other. No. Mrs Dixit was not frivolous at all. It was just that she wouldn't or couldn't draw a rigid enough line between what was generally considered good and what was generally considered evil. "Good is good," Kundan would say, "and bad is bad." But this was one point on which Mrs Dixit felt unable to give him her usually very willing wifely support. Somehow a person entered into it Mrs Dixit would feel and alter the whole of one's conception. A person with a certain background, a certain ideal and a certain compulsion. "There's nothing whatever about Bhadoo," said Kundan anticipating, from habit, her possible reactions, "that can be said to be a mitigating factor. He's an unspeakable rascal and he also looks it."

But the more she heard about Bhadoo the more difficult did she find it to conform to the general impression about him. She began to feel that her own ideas might be a little warped, for she could not help feeling a bit sorry for one so beleaguered by his own temperament. It was only a few weeks after they had moved in that Bhadoo became the subject of another scandal. She got it in devastating sequence from a number of people. It was at the weekly market, the Monday following the weekend she knew he had spent in the lugubrious company of his wife. She had heard all the fights, arguments, laments that marked the relations of the two and indeed she had to plug her ears with cotton wool for a time to shut out, not Bhadoo's, but his wife's shrill abuses. The woman had erupted suddenly into this querulous barrage till Bhadoo had said assuagingly, "Come on, come on, have some *bhang*," and they had both relapsed into some sort of coma for the day. "Yes," the people said, "They're both addicts, you know. You wouldn't believe it if you saw her. She looks so incapable ... of anything." He must have woken up with a vengeance. He had sauntered out to the market. But what a mistake he had made! He was caught plucking at the *pallus* of two women at the market. They had turned out to be the wives of respected local citizens, women he had never seen before but about whose manner for once his practiced eye had deceived him. He had mistaken the freedom with which they had moved about for the immodesty of their lesser sisters, When the crowd closed in to thrash him at the behest of the indignant husbands, the trader Jumna Lal and cinema proprietor Kukam Rai – alas, he knew them he had cried out, making matters even worse. "But I thought they were the local *Vaishyas*."

'If they had been, you scoundrel, you'd have known them."

"Help!" he had shouted when the first blow struck.

He had kicked aside the sacks of wheat that were ranged around him and fled, his fat stomach quivering like jelly. It had been a hot day and he had taken off his shirt and kept it by while his servant had fanned him: now he was seen running in a *lungi* and the grotesqueness of his fat and loose stomach bobbing up and down in such ludicrous despair had become too much for the crowd. It had lost its hostility and plunged into waves upon waves of mirth. The buyers had stopped buying, the little boys had stopped weaving in and out of stalls, the women had stopped haggling and the screaming and the shouting and the noise just stopped as the entire market gave itself up to uncontrolled merriment.

Bhadoo had run faster from the laughter. His vanity was hurt but anger and fear had alternated like uneasy masks on his face. He had wiped the sweat that flooded his eyes from the unaccustomed exertion and hurled imprecations over his shoulder as he ran.

It was only when he reached Urku's tea shop that he stopped to catch his breath. Urku of course was astonished, and this part of the story Rami got from Urku himself who told her maid servant who told her.

"Bring me a towel," Bhadoo had ordered. He had stood and wiped his steaming body but when it came to the legs he couldn't reach them for the stomach that stood in the way.

"Here, rub my legs," he had said brusquely to the servant boy in the shop.

The boy had sniggered and bent down to do so. Bhadoo whacked him on the head.

"That was my boy," Rami's maid servant added angrily in parenthesis.

"You'd smile, would you?" Bhadoo had expostulated, and then thrown a five rupee coin at the boy. "Go, get me two cigarettes from Anokhey."

The boy disappeared, and Urku had insisted tremulously overawed by Bhadoo as he usually was. "But w-what happened?

"The swines there. Send their women out like shameless wantons and then curse me because I take them for *Vaishyas* last time.

"Did you … er … I mean, was …"

Bhadoo cleared his throat roughly and spat through the door outside with the precision and crack of a pistol shot. "No, you fool, I didn't have time to do anything. Last time I brought one away. She was a beauty. Full figured and cheeky, not above sixteen. Those sons of pigs. They all know that at the Monday market the women come to be seduced, eh? You know, Urku, don't you?"

"No, no, I wouldn't dream of it, I couldn't …"

"Well, to be fair, some women come with that idea. But they shouldn't let their wives out if they're going to be so cussed – you should have seen those two. They were swaying like the seconds hand of the big clock in my verandah you've seen it, haven't you?"

Urku had nodded, his eyes hungry for details.

"You should have seen him," the servant boy had added his own account to that of his mother, he was so eager, his mouth watering, "Ah, and my own son?" his mother had rejoined, and the boy, only 15, had had the grace to blush.

"From side to side, like this," Bhadoo had continued, and cupped his hands so lascivously round empty space that he made it look as if it were the hips of a woman that he was fondling. He had looked thoughtful for a moment and then murmured. "Though I'd prefer, say, this size, and brought his hands closer.

"You know why, don't you, Bai Sahib? Why he made it smaller? Oh, the rogue, the wretched rogue that he is," the maid servant had exclaimed.

Poor Urku's eyes had steamed with excitement. He was

incapable of reading the nuances of Bhadoo's gestures but he was inflamed by assured references that Bhadoo made to the great subject of his confidences, women.

"Do you blame me if I found it irresistible? They should keep their bloody wives locked up in their homes to cook and feed the children. Has anyone ever seen my wife, eh? Have you, Urku? Can you say you have, eh?"

"No, no, no ..."

"You see, no chance for her to play dirty."

And then, God knows, what had come over the timid Urku that he said, in spite of himself, vaguely. "There's always the servant."

"Eh, what?"

"The servant, the s-s-servant in the – the h-house." he had stuttered, straining backwards in his chair.

"Mean fellow," Rami commented.

"No, no Bai. Its possible. You don't know what goes on in these big houses?" the maid servant insisted with that profound acceptance that marked her class. "You wouldn't blame the woman, would you? Imprisonment it is, nothing less. I wouldn't stand for it. Specially when my husband played around with others the way Bhadoo Bhaiya does."

"You did leave your husband, didn't you?" Rami asked her.

"To each his own," shrugged Sundari, "he found somebody better – so he said – so I let him go."

"And you?"

"I like it alone."

When Urku had made that remark about the servant, Bhadoo

seemed to have been shocked into silence.

The same night he beat his wife. Rami and Kundan heard him. "You bitch," Bhadoo had shouted, "from tomorrow you'll have only a maid in the house."

Well, that was that, thought Rami. She was glad it was all confirmed. He was as unspeakably disgusting as they said he was. It was such a relief to feel it wholly without doubts. He was bad, evil, cruel and she would be doubly wary. She didn't care about the women, how many or what he did nor even that he beat his wife – no, she did care. She couldn't forget the poor woman's face as she had called out about ten o'clock over the wall that divided their courtyards at the back and begged for some milk. "It - it - g-got spilt over and there's none for tea in the morning. Can you share some, *behen*?" One side of her face was swollen though she tried to keep it covered with her *pallu* and Rami didn't ask her about it. She just said while handing her the milk, "Oh, I'm dreadfully sorry." Perhaps the compassion in her voice was more than the spilling of the milk, warranted; the shrewish face across the wall seemed to soften and the tears welled up in the small, shrunken eyes. "Thank you, *behen*," said Bhadoo's wife, and disappeared from view.

For some time after that she didn't even see Bhadoo. Perhaps he was a little ashamed of that fracas in the market and deliberately kept out of the way. She never let Niloo alone anywhere and even her obsessive vigilance seemed to turn gradually into another one of her well regulated habits. Suddenly they heard that Bhadoo had gone off to Nagpur again. To the asylum. "He's given a special room, pretty nurses, they must be pretty, knowing Bhadoo," said Kundan, "distributes flowers, tips lavishly and makes himself rather popular generally. The doctors make a pretence of treating him. Perhaps they do. Perhaps he does talk of what matters to him. Anyway it seems this is the only time he can spend money on himself without being told off by his wife. Perhaps he too enjoys the relief of her absence who knows? I do." Kundan looked quite cheerful. "It's good to know the scoundrel isn't around." But their relief was short-lived. Two months later Bhadoo was back, and Rami heard it from the most unlikely source – Niloo. For a moment she had felt so weak with fright that she had had to sit down and her hand had flown to her heart to stop it from exploding out of her skin. "Ma, ma," Niloo skipped in suddenly waving her hands excitedly in the air. "Bhadoo *chacha* met me on the stairs and gave me this box of sweets. From Nagpur, he said, specially for us."

"Us?"

"He's waiting outside. He was shy to come in."

"Oh, God."

Before she could say anything, Niloo went and brought him in, holding him by the hand. Rami thought that contact was the most heinous she could behold. She felt her skin shrinking with distaste. "Niloo!" she screamed. Bhadoo took a step backward and his big, fat, childish face turned pale, "I'm sorry. I shouldn't have come in like this."

"No, no, please forgive me. I was angry with Niloo for going out. I h-had told her not to."

"Niloo is such a sweet child. She reminds me of what my own children used to be like", sighed Bhadoo, "before, before ..."

"Before what'?" asked Rami disarmed,

"Before my wife turned them against me," said Bhadoo simply.

The fellow was physically repulsive. But Kundan was mistaken. The face before her was not that of a rake and lecher, but of a precocious child gone wrong. A corrupted child. The knowing air went ill with the chubby innocence of feature and in a full grown man this was an offence ... to good taste. It put her off. But the creeping sense of tolerance she felt inside – was that not an offence? Shouldn't one take a stand against evil? He was standing at her doorstep. "Would you like a cup of tea?" she asked. His response was eager. As with a child you are continually nagged by the faith that things can never be irremedial, that behind the spoilt exterior must lie a basic vulnerability so with Bhadoo she felt this irrational belief that the man was basically good. But then weren't all men good in that way?

She couldn't help feeling sorry for him. In spite of everything – his vulgarity, the unforgivable beatings he gave his wife, the stories she had heard about his treatment of his children. If anything was wrong she argued to herself it must be with the whole family, the wife particularly the shrew that she was, and not with this childishly silly fellow standing in front of her and exuding such a thick air of sentiment.

"Please sit down, she said,"

She gave him some tea.

"It is perfect," he said. It is such a pleasure to have good tea.

Won't you teach me how to do it, Bhai Sahib? Then I can tell my wife."

"There's only one secret," she smiled, quite relaxed. "One has to make it with feeling."

"Feeling?"

"With love."

"Oh."

Bhadoo had never been entertained alone before by what he would term a woman of class. He couldn't ascribe any motives to Rami Dixit. Her figure and manner defied such an idea. But there he was safely ensconced in a modern looking drawing presided over by a woman of charm and intelligence. Poor Rami. She did not know that the remark about making tea with 'love' had set off the most amazing mechanism of emotion in the heart of the man sitting opposite her. He dared not, he absolutely dared not think that her attitude could stem from anything but the concern of a well bred woman for a sorry creature like himself. But he was overwhelmed. He cast shy glances at her. His heart was hammering inside him. He got up, his bulbous belly slithering like jelly and went towards her. Rami cowered in her chair. What had come over the man, the silly fool? But Bhadoo had no such intentions. How could he dare. She was like a goddess. He flopped down flat on the ground, all the full length of his body, and laid his head at her feet.

"I am your slave," Bhadoo said. "I will be your slave forever."

Rami Dixit felt the first faint rumble of disbelief tickle her stomach. Then the merriment began to mount up like a storm within her. She must stop it, she thought, but she could not. Her body shook and trembled, the tears streamed down her face as she sucked in gusts full of air to try and arrest the onslaught, but it came... peals upon peals of laughter that erupted from her body in uncontrollable spasms as she saw Bhadoo raise his head and his shocked, hurt, bulbous face swim before her eyes.

Contributors

Ipsita Roy Chakraverti, journalist, teacher, counsellor and painter, has worked tirelessly for bruised and battered women. In fact, she has been felicitated by the Japanese press for being a champion of downtrodden Indian women. The first and only Indian member of the Society for the Study of Ancient Cultures and Civilisations in Montreal, Ipsita is at present considered one of the foremost authorities on Wicca in the world. She has done extensive Wiccan therapy work in India and is a healer of repute. Ipsita is a recognised researcher into the properties and ancient usage of rock quartz. Some of her findings are considered to be breakthroughs by conservative science.

Shama Futehally studied English at the Universities of Bombay and Leeds and taught English and Cultural History at Bombay University and the School of Architecture, Ahmedabad. Her publications include *Tara Lane*, a novel published by Ravi Dayal (1993) and *In the Dark of the Heart: Songs of Meera* (HarperCollins International, 1994). Shama's short stories are included in *The Inner Courtyard* (Virago Press, 1990) and *In Other Words* (Kali for Women, 1992). Journals such as *Namaste* and *Kunapipi*, an international magazine of the arts, have also carried Shama's stories. Currently she is Associate Professor (Western Drama) at the National School of Drama, New Delhi and reviews regularly for literary journals.

Namita Gokhale studied at Delhi University and Lucknow, UP. She has been a consultant in a Japanese firm and at present writes regular literary columns in *The Hindu, Delhi Times* and other newspapers. Namita attended the Cambridge Seminar in 1999 and has visited a number of countries in Europe, America and Asia. Her publications include *Paro: Dreams of Passion* (1984), *Gods, Graves and Grandmothers* (1994), *A Himalayan Love Story* (1996), *The Book of Shadows* (1999) and *Mountain Echoes* (1998), an oral history.

Vandana Kumari Jena, a recipient of several scholarships and prizes, has worked as a lecturer at Lady Shri Ram College (1977-1979) and joined the Indian Administrative Service (1979) in the Orissa cadre. Her short stories have appeared in leading magazines and newspapers such as *Femina, Savvy, New Woman, Women's Era* and *The Statesman*. Vandana's poems have been published in *Femina* and *The Asian Age* and she has also written extensively for children in *Tinkle, Children's World* and *Target*. Currently she is working as Education Adviser in the Department for International Development, British High Comission.

Manju Kak, who wields her pen like a paint brush, is the author of two works of fiction, *First Light in Colonelpura* (Penguin, 1994) and *Requiem for an Unsung Revolutionary* (Ravi Dayal, 1996). In 1995 she received the Charles Wallace Fellowship for Creative Writing at the University of Stirling, two fellowships from the Department of Culture in Literature and Culture, and recently for the Breadloaf Writers' Conference. She has done research in the Kumaon Himalayas on *Women, Myth and Ritual*, and on *Woodcraft*.

Lakshmi Kannan, is a bilingual writer who writes in English and in Tamil. She uses the pen-name 'Kaaveri' for her writings in Tamil. She has presented papers on the gender issue, on the art of translation, on the power differentials in language and on the post-colonial literary scene in several national and international seminars at home and overseas. She has also attended literary programmes at home and overseas as an invited writer. Presently, she is an independent worker and is engaged in her writing assignments. Kannan writes poems in English, fiction in Tamil, and has translated extensively into English, her own works as well as the works of other writers. She has also widely published her critical articles in English. Lakshmi has translated and published her own work as well as the works of other writers into English. Four of her titles have appeared in English translations: *Rhythms*, *Parijata*, *India Gate and Other Stories* and *Going Home*. Besides novels, she has translated stories and poems for journals and anthologies. Some of her translated stories have appeared in *The Journal of South Asian Literature* (Michigan State University, Michigan, USA); *Stories from South Asia*, Ed. John Welch (Oxford University Press, Oxford UK); *Wasafiri: Caribbean, Asian and Associated Literature in English* (London, UK); *The Inner Courtyard* (Virago, London, UK); *In Their Own Voice: The Penguin Anthology of Contemporary Women Poets*, Penguin India; *Truth-Tales*, Kali for Women, Delhi; *Imaging the Other*, Katha, Delhi and in others.

Manju Kapur teaches English Literature at Miranda House, Delhi University. She is the author of *Difficult Daughters*, a novel which won the Commonwealth Eurasia region prize in the first novel category. Currently she is working on her second novel.

Madhu Kishwar, Editor of *Manushi* and Reader, Satyawati College, Delhi University has several awards and publications to her credit. She is the recipient of the Vidula Samman (1998) instituted by Vikas, an institution dedicated to the cause of education and knowledge, Calcutta, Prabha Puruskar (1997) and the Chameli Devi Jain Award (1986) for the best woman journalist. Some of Madhu's books include: *Off the Beaten Track: Rethinking Gender Justice for Indian Women*, Oxford University Press, New Delhi, 1999; *Religion at the Service of Nationalism and Other Essays*, Oxford University Press, New Delhi, 1998; Editor, *The Dilemma and Other Stories* by Vijaydan Detha, translated from Hindi by Ruth Vanita, Manushi Prakashan, 1997; Co-editor (with Ruth Vanita), *In Search of Answers: Indian Women's Voices from Manushi*, Zed Books, London, 1984. Also published in Japanese by Akashi Shoten, Shoten, Tokyo, 1990, third edition, Manohar, Delhi, 1996. Editor, *Women Bhakta Poets,* Manushi Prakashan, New Delhi, 1989.

Sukrita Paul Kumar is a Reader in English at Zakir Husain College, Delhi University. She has been a Fellow at the Indian Institute of Advanced Studies, Shimla (1987-1990), a British Council visitor (1994) and a recipient of the Bharat Nirman Award (1991), Rockefeller Award (1991) and research fellowship by the Shastri Indo Canadian Institute (1992). Sukrita's collections of poetry include *Oscillations, Apurna* and *Folds of Silence*, critical works such as *Man, Woman and Androgyny* and *The New Story* and translations of stories like *Breakthrough* and *Mapping Memories.* Her latest book is *Ismat: Her Life, Her Times* published by Katha, 2000. Currently she is busy with a major UGC project and was also Director, Translation Project for Katha.

Anuradha Marwah Roy teaches English at Zakir Husain College, Delhi University. Her first novel *The Higher Education of Geetika Mehendiratta* (New Delhi: Disha Books) came out in 1993. Her second, *Idol Love* (New Delhi: Ravi Dayal Publisher) in 1999. She has also written academic and general articles, poems, reviews and screenplays.

Raji Narasimhan, who writes in English, was a journalist before she turned to creative writing in the late 1960s. A work of literary criticism and the second of her four novels to date have been set texts in Indian universities. Her short stories have been translated into German and Gujarati. Her fifth novel, *Atonement* has been published recently. She is a regular translator from Hindi to English. In 1998, her translation of the novel *Nishkavach* by the well-known Hindi writer Rajee Seth, appeared in the Macmillan series, *Modern Indian Novels in Translation*.

Mrinal Pande writes in both Hindi and English. In English, she has two novels and a collection of essays entitled *The Subject is Woman* to her credit. Her first novel in English was *Daughter's Daughter* and *My Own Witness* is her most recent work. Mrinal has been editor of *Vama, Saptahik Hindustan, Hindustan Dainik*, and senior Editorial Adviser to NDTV (Star News). Currently she anchors Hindi news for Doordarshan and writes a column for *The Hindu* and *Punjab Kesri*.

Sujata Sankranti was born in a small town, Mavelikkara in Kerala.

Educated in Delhi, she is currently teaching in the Department of English, Sri Venkateswara College, University of Delhi. Her short story *The Warp and the Weft* was adjudged as the overall winner in the Commonwealth Short Story Competition organised by CBA, 1998. Subsequently the story was broadcast in all the Commonwealth countries and published in the journal *Commonwealth Currents*. The story has also been translated into Hindi, Malayalam and Urdu.

Bulbul Sharma is a Delhi based artist and writer. She has held several solo exhibitions of her paintings since 1987. Her works are in the collection of the National Gallery of Modern Art, Lalit Kala Akademi, Chandigarh Museum, British Council, UNICEF and the Nehru Centre, UK as well as in private collections. She has published three collections of short stories: *My Sainted Aunts* (HarperCollins), *The Perfect Women* (UBSPD) and *The Anger of the Aubergines* (Kali for Women). Her first novel *Banana Flower Dreams* was published by Penguin Viking in 1999. Her short stories have been translated into French and the novel into Italian. She has contributed to various anthologies which include *Something to Savour* and *Second Skin* (Women's Press, UK) and *In Other Words* (Kali for Women). At present, she is working on a series of nature books for children. Bulbul Sharma also works as an art teacher for children with special needs and conducts regular art and writing workshops for underprivileged children.

Madhu Tandan is a writer who, along with her husband, chose to abandon a comfortable city-life to join a small self-sufficient community in the Himalayas where they spent seven years. This experience inspired her first novel, *Faith and Fire: A Way Within.* She is currently working on her second book, *A Dialogue With Dreams*.

Uma Vasudev is an author, journalist, filmmaker and Director of In Group'80: The Media People. Her books include *Indira Gandhi: Revolution in Restraint, Two Faces of Indira Gandhi, The Song of Anasuya* (a novel), *Shreya of Sonagarh* (a novel) and *Issues Before Non-Alignment*. She is currently working on a book entitled *The Making of an Opposition,* a study of India's evolutionary pains as a parliamentary democracy. Uma's short stories have appeared in *Short Story International, New York, Hong Kong News* and in several Indian magazines.

Jehanara Wasi (General Editor), who holds degrees in History from the Universities of Delhi and Oxford, is a writer, editor and researcher. She has worked with such leading publishers as Oxford University Press, Macmillan, Vikas, Tata McGraw-Hill, Rupa and NCERT in Delhi, has been a literary columnist for *The Economic Times,* and a regular contributor to other papers on literature, history, the visual and performing arts. Her work has been published in *The Times of India, The Fountainhead, The Sunday Observer, The Hindustan Times, Indian Horizons, The Education Quarterly, Saturday Times, The Statesman, Travel Times, Vidura, Design, Destination Traveller, Indrama, Discover India, Swagat, City Scan, The Patriot, Link, The Financial Express* and *First City.* Currently Jehanara is engaged in documentation for *Span* magazine, research projects for international organisations and editorial assignments for Indian and foreign publishers. Several publications, both Indian and international, have been coordinated, evaluated and edited by her. She broadcasts frequently, is a regular script writer and presenter of programmes on All India Radio. External Services, English Talks and the National Channel and also voices commentaries for short TV films and documentaries. Jehanara takes on work in editing, re-writing and documentation and obtains detailed factual information for writers, academics, business consultants and administrators. She has evaluated examination papers and scripts in Creative Writing for the Indira Gandhi National Open University (IGNOU).